7 Secrets of Happiness
Your Brain
Doesn't Want You to Know

Second Edition

Kevin E Meredith

You may contact the author at
kevinemeredith@gmail.com

The First Edition
was published in digital form in 2012

This Second Edition
was printed in the United States of America

ISBN 13: 978-0-9984534-0-8

(v: 12/29/2016)

Book cover design by Scarlett Rugers Design
www.scarlettrugers.com

to all the consciouses,
as they at last come into their own

Table of Contents

Foreword

A little before 4 a.m. on a hot July morning in 2006, a woman I'll call Cynthia – furious to the point of insanity – picked up her cell phone and dialed my office number.

Her phone, a masterpiece of human ingenuity, initiated the call by broadcasting electromagnetic waves that represented a set of numbers unique to her telephone account. The waves reached a nearby cell tower and were identified by a local control channel. After a brief exchange of data, a mobile telephone switching office assigned Cynthia's phone the pair of radio frequencies that would carry the call.

Because I wasn't at my desk, it being quite early, the electronic impulses of Cynthia's call were rerouted to my company's computerized voicemail system.

After she listened to my greeting, heard my name and was prompted by a beep, another masterpiece of engineering prepared to operate: Cynthia's brain. Her mind, the product of billions of years of evolution, began accessing the mental library where the thousands of words in her vocabulary were stored. Then, with a speed far superior to anything current super computers are capable of, she began selecting from among these words, arranging, speaking and inflecting them in accordance with a complex set of logical and cultural rules:

> *"Hey, Kevin, this is [Cynthia]. You need to return my fucking phone call. I will find out who the hell you are. I will have you fucking arrested. Do you understand that?"*

As she spoke, her phone was converting her words, her tones, every pause and breath, into more than 100,000 ones and zeroes per second before sending them out at the speed of light through the early morning air:

> *"I do not know what kind of games you're playing because if you're some kind of sick fucking porn motherfucker, I will kill your sorry fucking ass, do you understand that?"*

There are a variety of definitions for insanity, and Cynthia probably met several of them as she left her message. And yet, while one area of her brain was gripped by a mad cocktail of fear, denial and rage, a second part of her brain continued, with exquisite recall and grammatical discipline, to assemble her next sentence:

> *"I will fucking take your ass out. Because you know what? I have a police officer as a husband. So you need to pick up your goddam telephone and call me because I will fucking take your ass out, you understand that?"*

I present Cynthia's call – a combination of the latest and most inspiring technology and some of the oldest and most frightening – to make the case that there's something very peculiar about people:

> *"I suggest you fucking call me back because I already have you fucking traced, I already fucking know where the fuck you live. I know everything about you. You understand that, you sorry fuck? You better call me."*

Cynthia, it should be noted, used some variation of the word "fuck" 18 times in her 70-second message. That's approximately one "fuck" every four seconds.

While the word has fallen into disrepute of late, its etymological parentage is likely as respectable as any other. It might have first been uttered in old Germanic, or perhaps Latin or Greek, and originally may have meant to strike or to plant or plow. But somewhere along the line, it got mixed up with human intercourse, and that was its undoing. Today, "fuck" lives exclusively in the red light district of the English language, leaping from the dark alleys of communication when there is pain, hate, rage, fear, or, oddly enough, intense physical pleasure.

Hear the word enough times and it becomes less an obscenity and more an object of curiosity, a four-letter testament to humanity's profoundly difficult relationship with itself.

Why are we so prone to fury? Why are we so ready to believe lies that bring us misery? Why are we so easy to exploit and abuse? Why are we so dumb? Why have we all been born with behaviors so completely out of place in a world of aircraft, modern medicine and smart phones?

Why is our quest for happiness so often thwarted – and why is it ourselves who are so often the thwarters?

It might be argued that understanding our angst has always been the most important thing humans could do, the ultimate purpose of any study of the human condition, from anthropology and history to philosophy and psychology.

We have, it might be argued, neglected the study.

Until now.

At last, hundreds of thousands of years after homo sapiens first began marching off the African savannah, the answers are within reach. We humans have finally achieved the level of scientific inquiry required to get a sense of what's eating at us.

This book attempts to present the most important discoveries in that vein, in a readable, perhaps even enjoyable way, with a particular focus on why we are so often so unhappy and how our brains secretly, oft *intentionally* contribute to that misery.

In the process of exposing our torment, this book will also offer prescriptions for what we can do about it as individuals. There's a great many options at your disposal, it turns out, once you understand what's going on.

Indeed, I'd like to imagine that, had Cynthia been a little more aware of humanity's long history of self-imposed suffering before she called me, she might have overruled her brain's furious, evolved directives and found something else to do that morning – saving me a little trouble and herself a great deal more of it.

After listening to Cynthia's message, I used my shaking hands to call the police. An officer arrived within 30 minutes, I played the recording for her, and she concluded that the crime of making a threat against another person had indeed been committed. Because Cynthia had provided her full name and telephone number in the message, the investigation proceeded quickly, and by the end of the day, a detective called to tell me what had happened.

Cynthia's son, I was informed, had been dialing a phone sex service and had racked up thousands of dollars in charges on Cynthia's credit card. She got the bill and confronted her son, and he told her someone had been calling *him*. Then he made up a phone number. My phone number. Cynthia, out lots of money and desperate to blame someone else for her son's transgressions, had apparently been trying to call me for hours, getting increasingly frustrated before she finally left her frightening message.

I pressed charges, Cynthia was arrested, pled guilty and apologized to me in a brief court hearing. She was fined and told to sin no more.

She was a single mom. There was no husband, certainly no police officer husband, and probably no capacity to harm me. It was all lies – what her son told her, what she told herself, the things she said in her message, and of course, the different sort of lie that was the telephone sex itself – cascading down one atop the other as they have tended to do throughout human history.

Unfortunately, the world is full of Cynthias, furious people believing lies and ready to kill over them. Some of them are single moms, and some are wealthy and powerful and well-armed. Some humans are Cynthias most of the time, but all of us are Cynthias now and then, doing harm – to ourselves and others – that doesn't have to be.

"Know thyself," instructed the Oracle of Delphi. Insofar as the brain encompasses who you are and how you experience the world, gaining a better understanding of your own brain's origin and design might be the ultimate fulfillment of the Oracle's advice.

I hope that you agree, and that this relatively short book will be helpful in that pursuit.

7 Secrets of Happiness
Your Brain
Doesn't Want You to Know

Introduction: The Mystery of the Eternal Pursuit of Nothing

Of all the strange things on strange planet earth, happiness must be the strangest.

Everyone wants happiness, from moment to moment and for all of life. We want it for ourselves and for everyone we love, for our children, our significant others, and sometimes even for total strangers.

"Happiness," insisted Aristotle in the 4th century BC, "is the meaning and the purpose of life, the whole aim and end of human existence."

There can be nothing more important to you than your happiness. If you lose everything but are somehow able to experience an abiding joy, you have more than most people. If you are rich, powerful, famous and miserable, you have nothing. Suicide is not uncommon among the supremely fortunate.

So constant and so determined is our pursuit of happiness that, if it were a mineral like silver, we would have long ago mined all of it from the earth's crust, built our cities with it, woven it into our clothing and probably learned to cook with it.

Happiness is not, unfortunately, like silver. It is more like Krypton 88, a colorless, odorless gas with a half life of 2 minutes 50 seconds.

There may be life elsewhere in the universe, but is there any place as strange as earth, where the planet's dominant species spends all its existence chasing something that cannot be reliably achieved? Indeed, after hundreds of thousands of years devoted to securing happiness through the glorious improvements which we today sum up as modern civilization, we humans seem to have arrived at a tragic and horrifying answer: Happiness is impossible.

Observed Randall Nesse in 2004:

> The triumph of technology over most of the specific causes of human suffering is nothing short of miraculous. But the deeper hope that this would lead to general happiness is not only unfulfilled, it is almost a cruel joke. Even among those who have succeeded beyond measure in getting what people always wanted, vast numbers of people remain deeply unhappy, and many of the rest live lives that feel frantic, meaningless or both. This is the core dilemma of modernity. What we have been doing to increase general happiness is no longer working, and there is no consensus about what we should try next.[1]

Similarly, from *The New Yorker*:

> A young filmmaker named Ricardo Costa . . . recently completed a short film (in which) he stands near the Astor Place subway stop (in New York City) with a camera and polls passersby. "I asked . . . are you happy. . . ? Some people said, 'I think so,' but they were not sure. Some people said that they didn't ask themselves the question, because they were afraid of the answer." The majority of New Yorkers told him, "Happiness doesn't exist."[2]

Shall we abandon the quest, then, and satisfy ourselves with merely existing among the fabulous technologies and immeasurable pleasures of modern life?

"Everything is amazing right now," observed comedian Louis CK, "and nobody's happy."[3]

Or might we pursue a new solution to what might very well be the greatest mystery in the universe? After all, we do have access to vastly more information and more science than any other generation of human beings ever. Might a few clues to the riddle of happiness lie among the knowledge of the modern world?

This book proposes that the answer is yes, that fascinating new discoveries about the brain, evolution and psychology reveal secrets to the persistent, ancient mystery of why – given our universal and lifelong pursuit of happiness – we are so poor at achieving it.

Among the points I will make in the coming pages:

- Happiness is elusive because it is designed to be elusive. You cannot always be happy, and indeed you must regularly suffer, for reasons that make perfect sense within the system of rules that created you.
- You are surrounded by lies and delusions created by another intelligence that resides secretly within in your brain.
- Your intelligence is strictly limited because it used to be dangerous.
- You see gods who aren't there, for reasons that used to make sense.
- You are easily exploited, in ways that are invisible to you.

In short, the legacy of the world where your brain and body were formed lingers on, controlling you in once-helpful ways that do nothing for your happiness – nor any good for the modern world.

And yet happiness can be had, I will propose, the deeper and surer kind that comes from understanding what you're up against, why life hurts and why it can sometimes be pleasant. I intend for this book to set out a radical re-thinking of what it is to be human, but it is also at its core a self-help book, a book whose primary mission is to make your life better through that strangest, most precious and most elusive of things: happiness.

What is happiness? Well, like art and pornography, people know happiness when they perceive it, and that's probably as acceptable a definition as any other. Happiness is feeling good. Happiness is the absence of pain. Happiness is an experience you want repeated.

Easy enough to define, but nearly impossible to achieve.

We are not to be blamed, you and I. We have come by our deficiencies honestly, all of us living embodiments of the difficult legacy of a world long past but maddeningly persistent.

Wherever we look in the human psyche and human behavior, we see the shadows of that ancient world, of a ghost that haunts us and too often robs us of joy.

Does the ghost have a name? What is his nature?

Secret 1: There's Someone Else in Your Brain: Introducing Your Ultraconscious

In this ambitious chapter, I will attempt the following:

1. Establish that you possess – and explain why you *must* possess – brain functions that aren't part of your conscious awareness or under your conscious control
2. List some of the more interesting and frightening behaviors of these secret brain functions
3. Provide the name, gender and overall disposition of these functions
4. Lay the groundwork for the rest of the book, in which I present the challenges to happiness, as well as the opportunities for happiness, that come with sharing your brain – and your existence – with such functions

When you're done reading this chapter – and if I have done my job well enough – you will have a new understanding of the invisible being that lives within you, and guides and controls you.

The being written of here is not a supernatural or spiritual being, I should quickly add, any more than this book is a religious work. I will offer wherever possible peer-reviewed science, and where I put forth theories that haven't yet been thoroughly researched, the arguments will be based on logic and, most often, the sort of research we are all doing in the process of living our lives.

Who's There?

Pick up a prehistoric human skull from anywhere in the world, and there's a decent chance you'll find something strange – a hole carved neatly through the bone. Evidence of ancient murder? Not necessarily. In a lot of these skulls, the openings don't look like acts of violence but seem to have been made methodically, sometimes by sawing four sides of a rectangle, sometimes by boring a series of small holes in a circle. Further, in many of these skulls, the bone shows signs of healing. In other words, the holes our forebears dug into each other's noggins with startling regularity were not violent acts of murder but instead made with such a clinical degree of care that the victim (or patient) lived on.

The idea of popping out a section of head bone seems to have occurred independently to people around the world. Evidence of treppaning, as the procedure is sometimes called, has been found on most of the continents humans have inhabited.

Why did they do it? While examinations suggest some of the procedures were done to cure a head injury or relieve internal pressure, researchers believe a good number of the incidents were meant either to let spirits out of the head, or allow then in. If true, these holey skulls serve as the physical manifestation of an idea that endures to this day: there's something else, or someone else, living within our brains.

The idea occurs in many forms and faiths, from the internalized animal spirits of shamanic religions to the demonic possession, divine guidance and spiritual channeling of such mainstream traditions as Christianity, Islam and Judaism.

All of us have surprised ourselves in doing something particularly stupid or out of character. "That wasn't me," we'll say. "The devil made me do it."

So, what else, or who else, is living in your brain and making you do things?

Writing in *How the Mind Works*, Steven Pinker identifies two "pools" of information processing in the human nervous system. The conscious pool includes "the products of vision and the contents of short-term memory," which are accessed to generate speech, rational thought and "deliberate decision making." Pinker's other pool "includes autonomic (gut level) responses, the internal calculations behind vision, language, and movement, and repressed desires or memories (if there are any). . . Information can sometimes pass from one pool to the other, but the transmission is limited."[4]

Other writers propose other metaphors. Anthropologist Pascal Boyer describes "a huge mental basement filled with extremely efficient servants, whose activities are not available for detailed conscious inspection."[5]

Psychologist and relationship therapist Harville Hendrix, offers this beautiful description:

> In the daytime, we can't see the stars. We talk as if they "come out" at night, even though they are there all the time. We also underestimate the sheer number of stars. We look up at the sky, see a smattering of dim stars, and assume that's all there is. When we travel far away from city lights, we see a sky strewn with stars and are overwhelmed by the brilliance of the heavens. But it is only when we study astronomy that we learn the whole truth: the hundreds of thousands of stars that we see on a clear, moonless night in the country are only a fraction of the stars in the universe, and many of the points of light that we assume to be stars are in fact entire galaxies. So it is with the unconscious mind: the orderly, logical thoughts of our conscious mind are but a thin veil over the unconscious, which is active and functioning at all times.[6]

Why would all this need to be there?

Well, consider how you are put together.

Your body is made up of trillions of cells – 10 trillion at least but maybe more like 50 trillion or even 75 trillion, depending on who's counting. These trillions of cells are organized into hundreds or thousands of varieties, to carry out the countless tasks that enable your survival. Muscle cells are keeping your body moving and your heart pumping. The cells of your stomach and intestines are specially designed to process food. Your blood alone is made up of a half a dozen types of cells. There are cells that make bone and teeth and skin, and other cells that enable you to see.

Right now, as you read these words, those trillions of cells are doing trillions of things, repairing damaged tissue, fighting off infections, producing and distributing hormones, enzymes, minerals.

Obviously, all these activities are taking place outside your conscious awareness, innumerable mysterious, microscopic processes you could not understand without an advanced degree in biology, chemistry and so forth, even if you could see them happening.

Now, imagine if that weren't the case, if none of your trillions of cells did anything until you consciously told them to. How long would you last? I would predict the failure of multiple major systems within seconds, unconsciousness within a minute and death quickly thereafter, from heart failure, the escape of stomach acids, the relaxing of vital muscles, the sudden unavailability of hundreds of essential chemicals. Even if you had the presence of mind to command your heart muscles to contract in something approaching a viable beat, literally trillions of other cells that must be doing their thing from second to second to keep you alive would stand idle, quickly failing catastrophically as they waited for commands that would never come.

Your conscious simply isn't equipped to run your body. The conscious is there to make the big decisions, where the body goes, what you think about, what you say, but none of that would be possible without trillions of tiny biological units living their own lives, making countless decisions and taking countless actions your conscious could not possibly manage.

Writing in *How the Mind Works*, Steven Pinker notes:

> "(Y)ou cannot tell me about the enzymes secreted by your stomach, the current setting of your heart and breathing rate, the computations in your brain that recover 3-D shapes from the 2-D retinas, the rules of syntax that order the words as you speak, or the sequence of muscle contractions that allow you to pick up a glass."[7]

It has to be this way. As one-celled organisms evolved into two-celled creatures, then multi-celled creatures and finally trillion-celled creatures, an increasing number of processes had to become automatic, completely outside the conscious awareness or control of the creature. Complex life is possible only if there is no awareness of and no need to control virtually all bodily processes. The relatively few cells you do get to control – most muscles, your diaphragm, your eyes and, to some extent, your thoughts – represent the thinnest veneer of everything you are and everything you're doing in this moment. Ten trillion cells, at least, are working tirelessly right now on projects you cannot perceive in any way in order that your conscious can read this book.

Truly, it's an inspiring thought: trillions of biological units have come together on this earth to serve only you, to take care of all your body's needs so that you can do whatever you decide to do from moment to moment.

Now, what about your mind? What's going on there that you also have no ability to perceive? The simple answer is – a lot. The sheer magnitude of brain resources and brain activities makes it just as impossible to manage as your trillions of bodily cells.

The Amazing Organ
The human brain is made up of at least 100 billion neurons, with an average of closer to 200 billion. That's billion, with a "b." Neurons, further, connect to and communicate with each other through synapses, and a single neuron can possess up to 10,000 synapses, or connections to other neurons. It is estimated that the adult human brain holds 100 to 500 trillion synapses. That's trillion, with a "t."

Impressed yet? Consider this: a synapse is capable of conveying numerous messages per second in the form of electronic signals. These action potentials, as they are called, represent an important part of the thinking that the brain conducts, and their aggregate power is staggering.

Writing in *IEEE Spectrum* magazine in 2008, science journalist and best-selling author John Horgan multiplied the number of brain synapses by the 10 electrochemical impulses per second each synapse might be able to transmit to propose that, at a theoretical maximum, "the brain performs 10 quadrillion operations per second."[8]

That's quadrillion, with a q. Written out, one quadrillion has 15 zeroes. It looks like this: 1,000,000,000,000,000.

Per second.

Inventor and futurist Ray Kurzweil went with 200 impulses per second, arriving at an even more impressive maximum possible number:

> The human brain has about 100 billion neurons. With an estimated average of one thousand connections between each neuron and its neighbors . . . With 100 trillion connections, each computing at 200 calculations per second, we get 20 million billion calculations (20 quadrillion) per second. This is a conservatively high estimate; other estimates are lower by one to three orders of magnitude.[9]

As Kurzweil acknowledges, the total number of operations per second is subject to widely varying estimates. So too is the number of those operations dedicated to conscious activity vs. the goings on of your non-conscious mind. We have no idea how many operations your mind must conduct to see each letter in this book, interpret them as words, understand the sentences formed by these words, process the larger ideas these sentences are trying to convey, and remember it all. It might take millions or billions or trillions of operations per second to do all that, but it's safe to say that a considerable number of your neurons and synapses, very likely the vast majority, are dedicated to doing other things, things you have no conscious awareness of, from directing your heartbeat to keeping your eyes blinking to making you fearful in dark alleys. This is the price you pay for belonging to the species with the biggest brain on the planet. Your brain gets a lot of things done from second to second, but you can't know about most of it, and you can't, for the most part, control it.

So what's your brain up to?

Let me answer that question with a question: The last time you saw something flying at your head, did you duck? And what prompted you to move out of the way? Did you consciously study the object as it closed in on your physical self, calculating its weight, speed and trajectory, then tell yourself, "Okay, I'll just move six inches to the right and close my eyes for good measure, and it will pass by harmlessly"?

No, you didn't. You simply ducked, without any conscious consideration. Assuming you ducked successfully, you have the non-conscious parts of your brain to thank. As the object made its way toward an unpleasant meeting with your head or body, that part of your mind took over. It didn't ask your permission, it simply assessed the threat, took charge of your muscles and forced them to contract in a manner designed to get you out of harm's way.

Now, stop and consider the words you just read: It didn't ask your permission. It simply *took you over and contracted your muscles.*

In that moment, even your large motor functions lay under the absolute authority of a being whose existence is completely separate from your conscious mind, a being unknown to you, a being whose life within your brain is lived invisibly, in the shadows.

Of course, if protecting you from flying dangers is all it does, great. But that's not all it does. This book has been written because there's much more being done without your permission. The non-conscious parts of your brain aren't just taking charge of your muscles during brief moments of danger – they're grabbing the controls of your mind constantly, ordering up feelings, ideas and behaviors for their own purposes, directing and fighting with your conscious in accordance with ancient, obsolete rules that have nothing to do with your happiness.

Naming It

So, what shall we call it, this other section of the brain, the part that operates outside your conscious awareness? Over the years, many names have been given to it, or to parts of it or aspects of it: subconscious, unconscious, id, heuristic processing, preconscious, system 1, homunculus, subliminal mind, collective conscious, non-conscious, archetype, hidden observer, old brain, hidden brain.

Look up any of these words or phrases on the internet and you'll find a wealth of definitions, concepts, philosophical treatises and new-age self-help movements, among them some that match the concepts in this book, some that do not. The word I choose therefore is not that important. Someday an expression, or more likely a group of expressions, will emerge as the accepted labels of the non-conscious aspects of the human mind, but until that time, those attempting to tell you about your secret brain will have to use whatever term seems to fit best for the purpose at hand.

I might go with "unconscious," which would probably win the most votes today. But "unconscious" offers only a root that means "not" tacked onto the word "conscious," making it the catchall term for everything that is not your conscious, including potentially silverware, goats, and the Milky Way. Worse yet, "unconscious" already has a clear meaning – the state of being comatose, asleep, knocked out or otherwise not conscious. It's rather like using the word "kaput" as the name for both all car engines and as the descriptor for a broken down car.

"Subconscious" might run a close second in a word election, but Freud himself dismissed the term as imprecise, and many feel it's so commonly and generally used it's meaningless. Plus, the prefix "sub," meaning below or inferior to, is not a good fit for such an important and powerful portion of your mind.

For my purposes, then, in this book, I use the term "ultraconscious," a term that has not yet entered common usage and still shows up as a misspelling in my version of Microsoft Word. "Ultra," furthermore, means both beyond our ability to perceive (e.g. ultraviolet, ultrasonic), and extreme (e.g. ultraliberal, ultraconservative), meanings that work well in capturing a part of your brain that you're not aware of but which controls the lion's share of your brain's operations.

Now, what gender should we apply, if any? I'm going with male in this book, for a few reasons. First, while I agree with the "he or she" convention for reasons of gender equality, it is an unnecessary encumbrance when no gender is going to be hurt by exclusion. Second, I prefer not to go with "it," because I want to convey that your ultraconscious needs to be thought of not as a thing, but in many ways like an individual, with his own concerns, preferences and ways of looking at life. Third, at the risk of sounding sexist, I believe that the ultraconscious, whether he resides in a man or a woman, has more in common with what we think of today as typical maleness. Men are more aggressive, more violent, more lustful, greedier, more often criminal, more powerful and more often the founders of new religions – all particularly noteworthy, troublesome and/or obsolete manifestations of the ultraconscious. There are of course countless and growing exceptions to the rule, on either side of the gender line, but for now, at least, in this book, your ultraconscious is male whether you are male or female.

(Now, a clarification. "Ultraconscious," like the words "government," "transportation" and "art," is a term that encompasses many things here. Humans invent such words to communicate more efficiently, but always at the expense of accuracy. The same is the case with "ultraconscious," and the many other words invented since the late nineteenth century to describe the non-conscious aspects of your brain. While the ultraconscious will be described most often here as a single entity with clearly-defined intentions, he might also be described as a mass of different parts, modules, systems, processes and such (a "Rube Goldberg device," it has been said) that do many, widely varying things, sometimes in concert, sometimes independently and sometimes in competition with each other. This is a book about you and your happiness first, so we will rarely delve into the fine points of ultraconscious complexity. This treatment should make the book easier to read but not, I hope, at the expense of an appreciation for how complex and diverse the ultraconscious truly is.)

So, now that you've been introduced – perhaps for the first time in your life – let's look at the evidence for his existence and what it reveals about his strange and frightening powers.

Behind the Veil: Catching Your Ultraconscious in the Act

So what's going on in that vast, secret part of your brain? The trillions or quadrillions of action potentials he can generate every second give him enormous powers, and science to date has only scratched the surface of them. Following is, briefly, a few of the most remarkable, bizarre or eye-opening findings about your ultraconscious:

Unconscious Activity. Researchers using the new technique of blood-oxygen-level-dependent functional magnetic resonance imaging (BOLD fMRI)[10] have found that the brain keeps operating in organized ways even when the person is asleep, in a coma or under a general anesthetic. "In the absence of external stimuli, activity persists," one group of researchers concluded.[11]

A group of British and Belgian researchers led by Adrian Owen, a neuroscientist at Britain's Cambridge University, used fMRI to scan the brain of a 23-year-old woman who had lain comatose for five months after suffering severe injuries in a car accident. "When asked to imagine playing tennis or moving around her home," the researchers wrote, "the patient activated predicted cortical areas in a manner indistinguishable from that of healthy volunteers."[12]

A team researching anesthetized monkey brains for an article in *Nature* in May 2007 notes that, even in non-human primates, "most of the brain's energy consumption is devoted to ongoing metabolic activity not clearly associated with any particular stimulus or behavior."[13] To put it more simply: "What's going on up there? We don't know, but it's a lot of something that doesn't seem to have anything to do with conscious activity."

The team adds, "coherent system fluctuations probably reflect an evolutionarily conserved aspect of brain functional organization that transcends levels of consciousness." Simplified again: "We have found organized brain activities in primates that aren't taking place at a conscious level, and we'll assume they got there through evolution because they helped these animals to survive and reproduce."

The discovery that the human mind is capable of non-conscious workings isn't entirely new nor dependent only on the latest technologies. A team of researchers using hypnosis in the 1960s found that people were able to perform calculations, hear sounds, feel pain and see while under hypnotic suggestions that rendered them deaf, blind or unconscious. "At a subconscious level there may be a process that is very like consciousness but not available to the open consciousness," they wrote. "The expression 'hidden observer' has been introduced as a metaphor to describe this concealed part that knows things that are not open to the ordinary consciousness of the person."[14]

Insight. In a July 2008 *The New Yorker* article, Jonah Lehrer deftly sums up a broad array of research being done to better understand the brain's ability to achieve an insight, that moment of brilliance when the solution to a complex or life-threatening problem arrives in your conscious all at once. Excerpts from the online abstract of the article make for a fascinating read:

> Mark Jung-Beeman, a cognitive neuroscientist at Northwestern University, has spent the past fifteen years trying to figure out what happens inside the

brain when people have an insight . . . He teamed up with John Kounios, a psychologist at Drexler University . . . The resulting studies, published in 2004 and 2006, found that people who solved puzzles with insight activated a specific subset of cortical areas. Although the answer seemed to appear out of nowhere, the mind was carefully preparing itself for the breakthrough. The suddenness of the insight is preceded by a burst of brain activity. A small fold of tissue on the surface of the right hemisphere, the anterior superior temporal gyrus (aSTG), becomes unusually active in the second before the insight. . . Earl Miller, a neuroscientist at M.I.T.. . . was able to show that (the prefrontal cortex) wasn't simply an aggregator of information, but rather it was more like a conductor, waving its baton and directing the players . . . It remains unclear how simple cells recognize what the conscious mind cannot. An insight is just a fleeting glimpse of the brain's huge store of unknown knowledge.[15]

A dramatic example of such insight is described by research psychologist Gary Klein, who tells the story of firefighters battling a kitchen blaze in a one-story home. Standing in an adjacent room, the team blasted the fire with water, to no effect. "Then the lieutenant starts to feel as if something is not right," Klein writes. "He doesn't have any clues; he just doesn't feel right about being in that house, so he orders his men out of the building. As soon as his men leave the building, the floor where they had been standing collapses."[16]

The fire wasn't in the kitchen after all; it was in the basement. "Had they still been inside, they would have plunged into the fire below." The lieutenant, Klein wrote, had no idea why he decided to leave the house. "(H)e said his extrasensory perception had saved the day."

When Klein reviewed the details of the incident, however, the true hero seemed to be not ESP or some other mystical force, but an instance of life-saving insight produced by the ultraconscious. As the lieutenant and his team sprayed water into the kitchen, his brain was assembling the clues his conscious hadn't noticed yet. Looking back on the incident years later, the lieutenant recalled that the room where they were standing was hotter than it should have been, that the fire was quieter than it should have been if its source were in the kitchen, and that the fire wasn't reacting to the water. The lieutenant didn't consciously know the home had a basement, but he didn't need to. In the invisible recesses of his brain, all the necessary information was being put together with remarkable speed, and then packaged up into a single instruction the lieutenant's conscious could quickly understand. "Get out now!"

Buried Memories. In the middle decades of the 20th century, Canadian surgeon Wilder Penfield and his associates treated epilepsy by cutting away the parts of the brain responsible for the seizures. They would prepare for this surgery by applying, while the patient was conscious, a mild electric current to the exposed surface of the patient's brain (which didn't hurt, since the brain lacks the ability to sense pain). The patient would sometimes respond to the stimulus by moving a certain body part or making a particular vocal sound, suggesting that the electrode was touching the place on the brain that controlled that particular behavior.

Sometimes, the patient would experience a very vivid memory. They'd hear a certain song as it was played by an orchestra, or they'd relive a conversation or some detailed incident from long ago. The memories were so vivid, the patients would often experience the emotions they felt in that earlier time. One patient remembered his friends in South Africa, and was once again, on the operating table with part of his skull removed, laughing along with them.[17]

Touching a place on the brain with the electrode more than once elicited the same memories each time, Penfield noted. The memories of particular songs, conversations or experiences seemed to reside at particular places on the surface of the patient's brains.

In a November, 1957, address before the Canadian National Academy of Sciences in Montreal, Penfield drew this remarkable conclusion:

> (T)here is, hidden away in the brain, a record of the stream of consciousness. It seems to hold the detail of that stream as laid down during each man's waking conscious hours. Contained in this record are all those

things of which the individual was once aware – such detail as a man might hope to remember for a few seconds or minutes afterward but which are largely lost to voluntary recall after that time. . . The record of this stream, as we have brought it to light with the stimulating electrode, might better be compared to the sequence on a wire recorder or to a continuous filmstrip with sound track.[18]

You don't need electrodes to uncover this ability, fortunately. The next time something seems vaguely familiar to you – a song, a few lines from a book or poem, a picture, or someone's name – think about how obscure the original memory was. Something you heard in passing 10 years ago? A piece of data you haven't thought about in ages? And yet the memory stayed within your brain, one of the countless files in the library of your ultraconscious.

Exposed Genius. In addition to the hidden mental capacities we all seem to possess, a tiny percentage of people have been born with a "flaw" that reveals exceptional brain powers that are usually kept hidden.

On June 18, 1980, researchers asked a 41-year-old Indian woman named Shakuntala Devi to find the product of 7,686,369,774,870 and 2,465,099,745,779. It took Ms. Devi, the daughter of a circus performer, a total of 28 seconds to multiply the numbers in her head and provide the answer: 18,947,668,177,995,426,462,773,730. Exhibiting extraordinary mathematical abilities from the age of three, and credited with many other feats of math and memory, Ms. Devi seems to be a prime example of someone whose secret calculative abilities are exposed to her conscious awareness.

Other members of this small group include those who instantly know the day of the week for any date, even thousands of years into the future, who never forget long strings of words and nonsense syllables, or who can recite detailed facts about any day during their lifetimes. There are child musicians who can play complex classical pieces after hearing them once, and artists who can create a precise representation of a scene they have glimpsed briefly.

Many members of this community are autistic. Richard Wawro, who sold more than 1,000 detailed, highly-accurate paintings – all reproduced from memory – was diagnosed as moderately to severely retarded at the age of three. He didn't learn to speak until the age of 11. Cataracts had rendered him legally blind.

Jill Price, an otherwise normal California woman studied for years by memory specialists, possesses a virtually complete memory of everything that's ever happened in her life, amazing researchers with her ability to recall endless details about news events, disasters and even the TV the specials that aired on any date decades before.

And yet, no significant differences have been found between the brains of these folks and the rest of us. Capable of performing calculation, transcription and memory feats many orders of magnitude beyond what most of us can do, their brain cavities are average-sized and the gray matter itself appears normal.

Thus, we might safely theorize that these brains aren't designed more powerfully but simply with a higher degree of access between the conscious and those incredible but usually hidden abilities of the ultraconscious.

Hidden Knowledge. The ultraconscious plays his cards close to the vest, his vast powers kept virtually invisible, but we have unmasked him in many ways. As described above, we have used high-tech brain scans and electrical manipulation. We have also merely observed in awe when confronted with that rare individual who does not forget, or who can complete staggering mathematical problems in seconds.

We have also exposed his abilities with some clever, albeit disconcerting experiments. For example, in the late 1970s, psychologists Ruben Gur and Harold Sackeim conducted an experiment in which a number of people with similar voices were recorded reading the same passage out loud. The recordings were played back to each subject, but with different voices making up different parts of the passage. The subjects were instructed to push a button when they heard their own voice.

Consciously, the subjects weren't all that accurate in identifying their own voices. *But something knew.* Each time their own voice was being played, even if they failed to press the button, their skin registered emotional arousal on a galvanometer. Used in lie detector tests and other types of physical monitoring, the galvanometer measures galvanic skin response (the electric resistance of the skin). When their voice played, the readings spiked consistently and significantly.[19]

In a similar experiment first performed at the University of Iowa in the 1990s, four decks of cards were placed on a table, and the subjects were asked to draw from them at random with a goal of maximizing their money. Two of the decks were blue, two red. Unbeknownst to the test subjects, the red cards were generally less valuable than the blue cards.

On average, by the time the tenth card was drawn, the test subjects demonstrated a heightened stress level, as indicated by the electrical conduction of the skin, anytime they reached for a red card. However, these test subjects had no idea they were responding this way and remained consciously clueless about the malevolent nature of the red cards. It wasn't until the 50th card had been drawn, on average, that the test subjects indicated a suspicion that the red cards were bad. And it wasn't until the 80th card or so that the test participants could actually articulate the reason red cards were a poor choice.[20]

In short, the ultraconscious knew by the 10th card there was a problem with the red deck, but he kept it to himself. The conscious didn't catch up with him until, on average, the 80th card.

In Review. Let's take quick stock of what we've discussed in this first secret, and then leap into that next, grim secret regarding what your ultraconscious thinks about your happiness (hint: not much). To summarize the main points above:

> **Conscious and Ultraconscious.** Your mind exists in two parts, a conscious and what will be called the ultraconscious in this book. The ultraconscious will be treated as a male individual here, not just a thing; his existence is most obvious when he takes over your body to force you to flinch and duck, but his influence extends far beyond that
>
> **The Brain.** The conscious and ultraconscious exist as roommates in your brain, an incredible organ that comprises 100 billion to 200 billion brain cells joined to each other in trillions of synapses which are together theoretically capable of something

approaching trillions or even quadrillions of operations per second.

Ultraconscious Activity. Scans of human and primate brains indicate considerable activity going on even while the conscious is asleep, unconscious or comatose. Among such identified activities are the processes that lead to insight, when multiple areas of the brain are activated outside your conscious awareness to generate important, even life-saving instructions, information and commands.

Buried Memories. The mind seems to store a detailed record of most or perhaps all experiences, an ability revealed most clearly when electric impulses are applied to certain places on the exposed brain..

Incredible Mental Feats. A small number of people possess incredible abilities for memory and calculation. Because the brains of such people are not unlike normal brains, we might assume they are simply better at consciously exhibiting the mental abilities kept hidden from most of our consciouses.

Hidden Knowledge. Subtle physical cues indicate that some part of the brain knows important things well before the conscious finds out.

We have a name, physical characteristics and a list of some of his more interesting abilities and behaviors. He is always awake while you must sleep for much of every day, and he knows far more, remembers far more and can think far faster than your conscious can.

Okay, you might be thinking, that's interesting. I've got a roommate in my brain who is very powerful and, by necessity, does his job in secret. It's a good thing he's on my side, keeping me safe and happy. Right?

Not so fast, unfortunately. Before we delve into the next secret, where we learn about your ultraconscious' involvement in your happiness, let's turn to his long and winding history. Where did he come from? How did he get into your head in the first place?

A Brief History of Your Ultraconscious

The history of the ultraconscious is a lengthy, undoubtedly interesting and mostly unknown one. But following are some of the things we have established, which I've broken up into four short sections:

Part 1: Animal Mathematics. In 2006, researchers in Germany and Switzerland began experimenting with the desert ant Cataglyphis.[21] They noticed that the ants seemed to know how far to walk to get back home from a food source, and they hypothesized that the ants were counting their steps.

Sure enough, when they cut some ants' lower legs off and extended other ants' leg with pig bristles, they found the ants next trips to be correspondingly confused. The ants with the longer legs walked too far. The shorter-legged ants didn't go far enough.

But the ants got used to their new legs on the next trip. Once they'd walked from the nest to the food source, all the ants – the longer-legged ones, the shorter-legged ones and the unmodified ants in the control group – took the right number of steps to return directly to the nest.

Further up the evolutionary chain, Sylvia Bongard and Andreas Nieder presented rhesus monkeys with paired images of dots and trained them to select the larger group. The monkeys were able to select the group with the larger number of dots more than 8 out of 10 times, the researchers found. And as they solved the problem, certain neurons in the prefrontal cortex fired consistently, suggesting that "single prefrontal cortex neurons have the capacity to represent flexible operations on most abstract numerical quantities."[22]

In an article about the research published by *HealthDay*, Nieder observed:

> Number crunching is a widespread skill among animals. So far, several mammalian and bird species have been shown to possess it, as well as salamanders, fish, and even bees. This ability has obvious survival advantages. In foraging, for instance, it is an advantage to choose the food source with more items compared to few. Also in social interactions, it pays to know the number of

individuals in one's own group as compared to an opponent party before deciding whether to flee or attack.[23]

Discoveries in the animal kingdom for working with numbers remind us that math isn't just a school subject that most of us find boring. Nor is it just an esoteric science that helps launch rockets and operate computers. Math is the stuff of life, as useful to ants as it is to engineers. With the ability to count and calculate, animals can measure distances, keep track of food supplies and census enemy populations.

Even plants do math, apparently, carefully consuming starch in the leaves overnight so they don't run out or have more than they need when the sun comes up the next morning.[24]

As the animal brain has evolved over the billions of years since life first appeared on planet earth, we may assume that the ability to do math evolved with it. Indeed, it makes sense that evolution, which has conferred upon earthly life the ability to see, to feel, to generate electricity, to glow, would also grant even the simplest creatures the ability to solve problems through mathematical calculations. And, once math was invented by evolution, we might logically expect it to remain a fixture in all subsequent brains, from the tiny ant brain to the relatively huge mammalian brain, all the way up to the brain you keep in your own skull.

The mathematical abilities we have uncovered in animals surely represent one of the strands of evolutionary development that ultimately became a part of the human ultraconscious.

So that's where the history of the ultraconscious might begin, with the development of complex mental capabilities, such as mathematical calculation, conducted so rapidly and in such vast quantities that they could not possibly be monitored or controlled consciously.

We might safely guess that other critical, non-conscious processes evolved in a similar way. The ability to store vast amounts of data, in the form of hidden memories, and to combine that data ultraconsciously at critical moments in ways that solved problems or saved lives, at some point found evolutionary favor and made their way into the human mind.

Part Two: Mismatch Theory. The capacity for ultraconscious memory and calculation did not evolve in a vacuum, however, and so begins the second brief section of this brief history of your ultraconscious. As the brain evolved the ability to calculate and remember and conclude, it did so in a world vastly different from the one you inhabit today.

And that's a problem, a serious deficiency that impacts your life every day, keeping happiness elusive.

Let me digress for a moment about dogs:

Before they lie down, dogs turn. Padding about flattens the grass, tests for thorns and tramps away snakes, scorpions and the like. Far better to have a paw stung or punctured, since you'll still have three good ones left while the fourth one heals, than to get a hole in your lung or venom in your neck. Turning was a good idea, so good in fact that even today, when a dog lies down on a hardwood floor or linoleum, it still turns.

If I were a dog, writing this book for other dogs, I would want my fellow dogs to understand this. "Do you still really need to turn to be happy?" I would ask. "The desire to turn before lying down is a behavioral feature embedded in our brains by evolution when all our world was grass. But we have paved and floored over the grass, and now turning is a waste of time and energy, not to mention dangerous. Mothers, how many of you have stepped on your puppies because you couldn't lie down without turning?"

Dogs that live in modern households act in accordance with ancient, evolved rules that once aided survival and reproduction but no longer do. Evolutionary psychologists have a simple term for the difficult condition of possessing a mind or body evolved in a different world than the one you now occupy: mismatch theory.

Dogs, of course, aren't the only victims of mismatch. The ancient world is the crucible where your mind, your emotions, the very thought processes you are using right now, were forged, and these mental phenomena are profoundly mismatched with the modern world. You can take the genome out of the jungle, it might be said, but you can't take the jungle out of the genome. The outcome of mismatch is sometimes amusing or interesting, and I will be sharing examples of both in this book. But the outcome too often is also miserable, as we react to events and situations in unhappy ways that used to make sense but no longer do.

"Human anguish in modern minds," writes David Buss, "is tethered to the events that would have caused fitness failure in ancestral times."[25]

In a 2011 email exchange with Canadian anthropologist Jerome Barkow, he wrote to me of "the adaptive value of unhappiness – sexual jealousy, loss of self-esteem in competition, our constant anxiety about our reputation and what others think of us, how we feel when our coalition (the team we root for or are part of) loses, the relationship between paralyzing depression and unhappiness that is a motivator, making us get up fighting."

Such pains were surely quite beneficial in ancient times, when there were very few mates around, reputation was essential to your success in many areas, and the loss by the clan in a fight over land or other resources might mean death. Today, most of the groups that we belong to or teams we support can fail with virtually no impact on our quality of life. As for jealousy, if your significant other appears to be interested in someone else, a serious conversation is in order, but certainly not the rage or hysterical despair we often hear about as a romance dies. The modern world is full of new lovers.

Does our intelligence make us the creatures on earth (or in the universe?) most susceptible to pain and pleasure? Bjorn Grinde wrote in 2002, "It is tempting to speculate that positive and negative sensations have a greater impact on the adaptation of humans than they have on any other species . . . (T)he capacity for self-awareness presumably evolved further in humans than in other animals. (A)s a consequence, we have more conscious appraisal of how we are doing."[26]

Mismatch between your ancient, evolved mind and the world you occupy today is not a death sentence for your happiness, however. If you can understand the evolutionary legacy that persists in your head, you can take a hard look at how it affects your life and your happiness, and you can counter it in your thinking and behavior. And in the process, your happiness very well might grow.

That, in a nutshell, is what this book is about. We will look at the ancient world and the kind of brain it might favor, and we will look for the things such a brain does today that no longer work.

Because this is a book about your happiness, we will direct particular focus on the ways your brain keeps you blind to happiness, hijacks your conscious pursuit of happiness, and allows others to define – or outright defy – your happiness.

The first step in such a project is getting a sense of life in the world where your brain evolved, so here begins the third brief chapter in our brief history of the ultraconscious.

Part Three: The Crucible of the Ultraconscious. So what kind of place was it? In what sort of world did the human brain evolve and, most importantly, how was it different from the modern world? How mismatched is the modern pursuit of happiness with the ancient, evolved brain you must use to conduct that pursuit?

It's too easy to forget that life hasn't always been the way it is right now. The logical value of the ways of modern humans are so obvious we are at risk of dismissing all that came before as just an embarrassing, brief and quite forgettable prelude to our ultimate destiny. For example, as you read this book, how often have you pondered the miracle of reading? Homo sapiens emerged in Africa hundreds of thousands of years ago. Only in the last few thousand years did humans devise a written form of language, and only in the last few hundred years have we developed the efficient mass-production or (much more recently) the electronic distribution of written works, coupled with the luxury of mass education, to achieve near-universal literacy. All the time before that, our knowledge was limited to what we observed and what we were told by the small number of people who could and would speak to us.

We all worry about being robbed or suffering a violent crime, but when is the last time you worried that your neighborhood or home would be invaded by another tribe, that you or your loved ones would be murdered as you slept by your campfire, that you and yours would be forced to flee in the night, losing all but the clothing on your backs, never to return?

One school of historic convention insists that life before agriculture (which began about 8,000 BC) and advanced civilization (which got its start a few thousand years ago) was a joyous Eden, full of contented, gentle, hunter gatherers living in a world of plenty.

I belong to the opposite school, the school that is certain life in prehistory was plagued by shortages of everything – food, shelter, mates, live births, medical care, clothing, shoes, safety and peace. In brief, as philosopher Thomas Hobbes wrote in the 17th century, ancient life was "solitary, poor, nasty, brutish and short."

It is beyond the scope of this book to argue the point to any great degree,[27] but a few facts are worth noting.

To start with, we have the pattern that all species follow. Invariably, each creature breeds to fill its environmental niche until the space and resources of the niche are used up. Bacteria do it, filling their hosts to the point of death. Deer do it, overbreeding in forests where there are no predators until die-offs return their numbers to sustainable levels. Lemmings do it, flooding their environment until its exhaustion triggers their proverbial mass migrations. And humans certainly do it, and probably always have, today using up fossil fuels, metals, water, arable land, rain forests, fisheries, old growth forests, clean air, wetlands and so many animal species that we have given the calamity a name, the "Holocene Extinction Event."

We've even begun using up outer space. The National Aeronautics and Space Administration was reported in year 2000 to be tracking almost 9,000 satellites and other pieces of manmade, orbiting space junk.

The human brain, the brain you carry about with you in your cranium every day, evolved in a fearful, desperate, oft-overcrowded place, a world it did not understand and had very little hope of learning more about. As the human and pre-human brain evolved, those mental characteristics that equipped one for life in such a place would be favored, no matter how irrelevant they might become in the world clever humans, even then, were starting to build.

Commensurate with the challenges of survival in ancient days were the many difficulties of reproduction, from finding a suitable mate to giving birth to raising an infant to seeing that child through to successful adulthood. Polynesian cultures still treat as a grand event the first birthday, so unusual was it for a new life to last that long. If one were to successfully reproduce in the world before today, one had to be both profoundly lucky and very determined.

All of these characteristics of humankind's ancient, formative years – the brutality, the lack of knowledge, the fear and desperation, the difficulty reproducing – have left on your brain their indelible marks. "Scars" might not be too strong a word.

And now we reach the final part in the brief history of the ultraconscious – and the end of our first secret, in which you have been introduced to your ultraconscious. Here, I bluntly ask, what are you?

Part Four: You. What does this book mean by "you?" It may seem that I am making a lot of assumptions as I compare you to the ancient people from whom you have inherited your brain. But if you are reading this book, I do know a great deal about you, and I am certain there lies a vast gulf between you and your distant ancestors.

First, you are literate, a fact that separates you in fundamental ways from everyone who lived before the first alphabets were invented a few thousand years ago, and a few thousand years is but an eye blink in your genetic legacy. Remember that your human and slightly pre-human ancestors have been adapting to this earth in an illiterate fog for millions of years.

Second, you are spending precious time reading. Not fighting enemies, gathering food, huddling in the dark or trying to start a fire. The fact you have the free time to do something so unessential to immediate survival makes you very different from the people whose evolution brought you into the world.

Third, you are reading a self-help book, a presentation of information based on science, fact and logic that will hopefully improve your quality of life, your self-awareness and your understanding of others. Your interest in this topic and your ability to understand it as presented here speaks volumes about how irrevocably different you are from virtually all your primitive forebears.

Picking up, reading and understanding a book of this sort requires decades of instruction, training, practice and curiosity, a virtual re-engineering of important areas of your brain that never took place in the brains of those from generations past.

Indeed, modern human behaviors are so different from those of our forebears – and from the behaviors that evolved to keep us merely alive and reproducing – that some researchers use the word "parasitic" to describe modern humanity. Our capacities for art, music, literature, science and so forth are unjustifiable from an evolutionary standpoint, constituting behavioral mistakes or by-products – misuses, in other words, of the things our brains were designed for, in the same way that a tick represents a misuse of its host's blood.

If we define as human that species designed for life in the world we occupied for most of our evolved history, you are barely a human being. Neither am I. This is not an insult.

How Understanding Secret 1 Might Make You Happier

People have long suspected there was someone else or something else living in their brains, but it's taken modern science to confirm the presence of that other, uncover his behaviors and capabilities, and offer ideas about what he wants.

The unmasking of the ultraconscious has proceeded quietly over the last century or so, typically through scholarly papers and esoteric experiments the general public doesn't have time to read about, but it is arguably one of the most important discoveries humans have yet made – in any field. You simply cannot say you know yourself until you know of this other, and this knowledge is inescapably life-changing. But is it the kind of knowledge that is also happiness-changing?

By itself, probably not. The knowledge of the presence of that secret other is not in itself a cure, any more than knowing you have cancer is in itself a cure. Knowledge is the best first step to a cure, however, and knowledge is what this chapter has attempted to deliver.

Up next, we delve more deeply into your ultraconscious' relationship with your happiness. Does he want you to be happy, or not?

Secret 2: Your Ultraconscious Doesn't Want You to Be Happy

Of all the difficult secrets in this book, this is surely the most difficult. Happiness, understood as the goal of all humanity through all our long history, isn't actually your goal.

"(N)atural selection never promised us a rose garden," asserted Robert Wright in *The Moral Animal*. "It doesn't 'want' us to be happy. It 'wants' us to be genetically prolific."[28]

If you are the total package of your body, your conscious and your ultraconscious, the goal of that total package is something other than the pleasures of life experienced by your aware, awake self. You might think your first objective is the pursuit of happiness, but most of your brain secretly disagrees. If you want to be happy, or happier, it is absolutely essential that you understand what you're up against.

Here's how Randolph Nesse has described the challenge:

> We were not designed for happiness. Neither were we designed for unhappiness. Happiness . . . is an aspect of a behavioral regulation mechanism shaped by natural selection. . . Natural selection has no goals: it just mindlessly shapes mechanisms, including our capacities for happiness and unhappiness, that tend to lead to behavior that maximizes fitness. Happiness and unhappiness are not ends, they are means.[29]

Nesse offers no apology for what he writes, but he does admit to the difficulty of these ideas, particularly to any reader who believes in the most popular happiness myths: We are put here for happiness; we will achieve permanent happiness if we just work hard enough for it; happiness is the natural state of things, and anything else is unnatural.

"The utter mindlessness of natural selection," Nesse observes, "is terribly hard to grasp and even harder to accept."[30]

Happiness was favored by evolution not because it gave us something to enjoy and live for, but because it was an effective tool for getting the conscious to do what the ultraconscious wanted – and what the ultraconscious wanted, because evolution selected these wants over the ages, was survival and reproduction. You exist today, reading these words, as the end product of a long, unbroken line of evolutionary parentage in which evolution was invariably in favor of those creatures who survived and had offspring. Were they happy? Who cares? They didn't survive and reproduce because they were happy, so evolution had no use for happiness as an experience unto itself. Instead, evolution used happiness as the reward for surviving and reproducing, and it used something other than happiness as the punishment for doing what ran counter to survival and reproduction. You would not exist unless all of your ancestors did their part in conception, and they in general played their role in reproduction because it made them happy to do so (in general, although not necessarily true in every instance – sex and children are sometimes forced on people – but the billions of people alive today suggest that for the most part, people like reproducing).

Long ago, some relatively advanced creature was born with a new mutation that caused it to consciously experience a psychological phenomenon it found gratifying. It was all just a trick of chemicals, a new sort of squirm among the brain cells, but the creature knew none of this. Its conscious knew only that a good thing had happened, and that it wanted it to happen again.

Evidence indicates that reptiles were the first to be aware of the rudiments of happiness, in the form of pleasant and unpleasant sensations. Writes Bjorn Grinde:

> There are data suggesting that this awareness (of happiness) evolved between the amphibian and reptile stage of vertebrate evolution: A reptile *seeks* pleasurable stimuli, such as sunbathing; and it is actually possible to measure a physiological response in the sunbathing reptile akin to what can be

measured in humans who engage in positive experiences (Cabanac, 1999)[31]. Fish and amphibians do not show the same physiological response; their behavior is presumably more instinctive and less influenced by an appraisal of sensations.[32]

Perhaps the happiness mutation as it arose in those ancient reptiles sometimes awarded happiness randomly, like a broken clock that gonged at odd times. Or perhaps it granted happiness in response to something not in the creature's best survival or reproductive interest. Happiness was being out in the open, perhaps, where a predator could get it, or happiness was being alone. These creatures might have lived happy lives, but they were short happy lives. They did not breed, and their inappropriate happiness gene died with them. But evolution got happiness right often enough that it became a fixture in our minds, permitting its experience only under those circumstances where, from the perspective of reproduction, the right thing had first been done: the acquisition of food, victory over a rival, mating.

Your brain, the result of millions of years of soulless evolution, *does not want you to be happy*. But *it will permit you to be happy* if the right conditions are satisfied.

Evolution invented happiness for its own inevitable purposes, purposes we are only now beginning to understand. So we can lament the dark and deceptive purpose of happiness, or we can decide instead to celebrate its existence, regardless where it came from, to grab more of it and, ultimately, have the last laugh.

In the fairy tale, Hansel and Gretel are abandoned in the woods by their stepmother. Lost and hungry, the children wander hopelessly until they come upon a house made of gingerbread and candy. They set upon it with delight and soon meet the home's owner, an elderly, seemingly kind woman. Soon enough, however, Hansel and Gretel discover the old woman's true intentions. An evil witch, she enslaves Gretel and imprisons Hansel with the plan of eating him.

The gingerbread and candy home, and the happiness it represented, was all a lie, a trick to lure the children. But the witch's evil plot doesn't make the house bad, any more than our ultraconscious drive to reproduce makes happiness bad. It's just that, before the house or happiness can be understood and truly enjoyed, we need to understand where they came from and what challenges they present.

Hansel and Gretel understood that their challenge was a witch, so the story goes, and they overcame the difficulty by pushing her into an oven (None of the versions of the story I've read say what happened to the house after the witch was out of the picture, but I'd like to think the kids set upon it with renewed gusto, biting off chunks of wainscoting and door jambery without concern for its source).

Our challenge is a great deal more complex, but not insurmountable. Instead of a single person, we face billions of brain cells, scheming ultraconsciously, performing uncountable operations every second to make us feel, believe and do things that sometimes make us happier, and sometimes sadder. There's no one we can push into an oven, but there is much we can do to understand and fight the enemy that stands between us and happiness.

Once again, Robert Wright puts it helpfully: "(W)e're all puppets," he writes, and "the puppeteer seems to have exactly zero regard for the happiness of the puppets . . . (O)ur best hope for even partial liberation is to try to decipher the logic of the puppeteer . . ."[33]

This book was written to present the motives and methods of the puppeteer, as well as to counter them. But what can you do? You cannot swap out the brain evolution labored so long to give you, any more than you can swap out your legs for a pair that runs faster or supports more weight.

Your brain, however, like your permanent pair of legs, can be exercised and improved. Your brain is actually quite malleable, surely the most changeable of all your organs. Where it takes weeks of exercise to strengthen muscle and bone, the operations of the mind can be altered in an instant, with a single idea. You can learn, gain new perspectives, better your responses to the challenges of life. You can be born again. This book was written in the humble hope it might help you in that process.

In the same way that Hansel and Gretel's witch disguised her evil intentions behind a gingerbread and candy house, your ultraconscious hides his single-minded agenda for your reproductive success behind a wall of emotions, beliefs and involuntary thoughts, and until you learn to see him and perceive his wiles, your pursuit of happiness is nothing more than the futile chasing of dreams and illusions.

"Got it," you might be thinking. "I have an evolved ultraconscious who gives me happiness only when I do what he wants me to do, like succeeding, acquiring and mating. That's pretty harsh, but I guess I'll have to live with it. And if I'm better than average at keeping my ultraconscious satisfied, I ought to end up happier than average. Right?"

Not necessarily. I have so far offered only the grim view of happiness generally accepted among evolutionary psychologists, where happiness is not the end, but merely the means to an end. In the next section, I will offer evidence and arguments for a theory of mine that goes to a darker place, that proposes that the system isn't based just on rewards for doing that which satisfies your ultraconscious, but that you are meant to live out your entire existence pursuing a form of happiness that doesn't exist.

The Cruel Necessity of Balance: A Theory

(Author's note: for a more detailed, comprehensive outline of this theory, see my book *Heirloom of Agony*[34])

Plenty has been written about the mind's ability to bring relief during times of pain, stress and deprivation. Most people can tell a story from their own lives, or of someone they know, who had a sudden feeling of hope, joy, even ecstasy, during a particularly difficult time. Pleasure-giving endorphins, released in the brain during orgasm, are also doing their thing during pain, injury, even strenuous exercise. In times of great suffering, acute stress reaction shuts down the mind altogether, and afterwards, memories of trauma are repressed, closed off from the conscious.

Much less (possibly nothing) has been written about the corollary, about the mind's inclination to inflict pain when times are good, but it is a feature of the human brain that must be fully considered if we are to pursue happiness with a complete understanding of what we're up against.

Let me begin by stating the obvious: happiness is cyclical. Sometimes you are happy, sometimes sad. Life goes up and down. It's a concept as old as humanity, captured long ago by the Wheel of

Fortune, a myth based on the universal understanding that lives must change, that the poor and downtrodden will rise and that the great and famous will be brought low. In the Roman version of the myth, the goddess Fortuna controlled the wheel.

"The wheel is turned by Fortuna," warned the 12th century poet in *Carmina Burana*. "I go down, demeaned; another is carried to the height; far too high up sits the king at the summit – let him beware ruin!"

Evolutionary psychologists have explored the idea more scientifically and arrived at ideas that support the old poetry. Our happiness waxes and wanes, as it must. Should someone be born whose genetic makeup allowed for constant happiness, that person could not be prodded with the goad of pain or the reward of pleasure, and they would thus lack one of the strongest reasons for doing what must be done for the sake of survival and reproduction.

"Perpetual happiness would have led to highly maladaptive, disorganized behaviour," writes Jerome Barkow, "the same reaction to a threat as to a friend or mate, the same reaction to a poison as to a food, the same reaction to a barren landscape as to one replete with indicators of food and drink (e.g., trees, flowers, streams or lakes)." Adds Barkow, "Perpetual orgasm would have led to a quick demise at the hands of predators, rivals, or simply as a result of dehydration."[35]

So we cannot be happy all the time. Fair enough. But what if life is good all the time? What if your spouse and kids love you, everyone's attractive, your job's going well and you have plenty of money in the bank? What if, in short, you are doing everything your ultraconscious could want not just to survive but to reproduce with flying colors?

That's a problem, we might argue, a problem evolution has had to deal with in a cruel but quite logical way. No matter how good life might be, I theorize here, your ultraconscious will inflict pain on you in order to keep you balanced. In fact, I propose, the better your life is, the harder your ultraconscious must work *to inflict artificial misery*.

You must be kept balanced between pain and pleasure so that you will remain maximally sensitive to the next reward or punishment your ultraconscious imposes, and a key strategy for maintaining that balance is the imposition by your ultraconscious of spontaneous, artificial pain when you are too happy.

We know that your ultraconscious can take control of your muscles, without asking your permission, in order to move you in the precise ways necessary to dodge a hurtling object. We also know that the ultraconscious can reward you and punish you, instantly and without permission, for the things you do that relate to survival and reproduction. You don't, after all, consciously instruct yourself to be happy when someone you are romantically interested in agrees to spend time with you. It just happens, a gift of the ultraconscious. And you don't decide consciously to feel blue when your property is stolen or someone insults you. The rage or sorrow is immediate and irrevocable, forced upon you by the ultraconscious even if the stolen property is insured or the insult is a few seconds of nonsense from the mouth of a deranged stranger. Pain and pleasure are rationed by the brain. That's a given. So indeed, the theory that rewards and punishments are meted out by the ultraconscious for no other reason than to help you maintain your emotional balance is just an extension of the concept. But it's an important extension, for it proposes a powerful obstacle to happiness among the evolved creatures called human beings.

It's also an idea with countless instructive examples, from the Bible to the gossip rags. I'll present a handful of such anecdotes below, but I invite you to write the next words yourself, in your own head, with a few questions: When life is going well and you are happy, how long does it last and how does it end – when the next bad thing happens, or from within, when an unpleasant memory, a worry, a sad idea or just a general gloominess lands like a thud among your billions of gray cells? And when life is bad, are you mysteriously sustained by positive thoughts that come from nowhere – happy memories, a hope in improvement, belief in a supernatural power's concern for you, or just a general uplift, as if someone has handed you a shot of joy juice?

I have tested the theory in my own life and mind, and found its manifestation consistent to the point that I know where much of my pain and pleasure comes from, and can sometimes even predict the next gift of a carrot, or the next swing of the stick before they arrive. A positive feeling will invariably be followed by a proportionate sting – often within minutes – in the form of irrational shame over some ancient failing, or worry over something that might happen, or a sudden shadow in the mood. Sometimes the pain is physical, a dreadful migraine that, as often as not, follows great joy. On the other hand, in the midst of difficulties, I will find regular respite, often in the form of the beauty around me that otherwise goes unnoticed. I haven't found a way to counter the process, but having a theory to explain what's going on has itself been a source of relief.

Such a system, managed not by the goddess Fortuna but by your ultraconscious, might also explain how humans, who are all born with the same number of chromosomes and made of the same stuff, can feel joy in a prison or a slum and misery in a waterfront mansion.

A simple experiment with water can illustrate the concept. If you dip your left hand in ice water and your right hand in hot water for a minute, then place them both in a pot of water at room temperature, that water will feel very different to your two hands – hot to your left hand, cold to your right – until they readjust. Like your hands, your brain adapts to its environment, quickly declaring your existence to be normal no matter how many pains or pleasures you experience each day.

If such a system is at work in your mind, we might argue that a great deal of what you feel from day to day in fact has nothing to do with what is actually good and bad in your life, but is simply an illusion conjured by your ultraconscious to keep you maximally sensitive and emotionally balanced. As John Milton wrote in the 17th century, "The mind is its own place, and in itself, can make a heav'n of hell, a hell of heav'n."

Bipolar disorder might represent an example of the mechanism run amok.[36] Sufferers of the condition (previously known by the more descriptive but now pejorative "manic-depression") swing from deep depression to a manic state characterized by grandiose plans, promiscuity and elevated self-esteem. Often, there is no cause for the swings. They simply happen, apparently under the direction of brain structures and chemicals that have – quite literally – a mind of their own.

But even for humans with normally functioning minds, the brain seems able to apply pain on a whim, regardless what has just happened. Aaron T. Beck, the psychiatrist who helped develop cognitive psychology, discovered that his patients "experienced streams of negative thoughts that seemed to pop up spontaneously." Beck called these mental events "automatic thoughts" and placed them in three categories: negative ideas about themselves, negative ideas about the world, and negative ideas about the future.[37]

Fear and worry without an identifiable cause is also common enough to have its own name: free-floating anxiety, defined as "a generalized, persistent, pervasive fear that is not attributable to any specific object, event, or source."[38]

An interesting story recounted by Antonio Damasio reveals the presence – and the staggering power – of one mechanism for inflicting pain. Electrodes had been placed in the brain of a woman with Parkinson's, but one of the electrodes was mistakenly connected to the wrong area. As soon as the electrode was turned on, Damasio writes:

> The patient stopped her ongoing conversation quite abruptly, cast her eyes down and to her right side . . . After a few seconds she suddenly began to cry. Tears flowed and her entire demeanor was one of profound misery. Soon she was sobbing . . . she began talking about how deeply sad she felt, how she had no energies left to go on living in this manner, how hopeless and exhausted she was . . . Her words were quite telling: "I'm fed up with life. . . I no longer wish to live, to see anything. Everything is useless . . . I feel worthless."[39]

The electrode was quickly turned off. "About ninety seconds after the current was interrupted the patient's behavior returned to normal." Damasio writes. "The sobbing stopped as abruptly as it had begun."

So, the mind has a demonstrated knack for making us hurt, sometimes spontaneously, sometimes through identifiable mechanisms. That doesn't mean the quest for happiness is futile, just that it must be conducted thoughtfully, and realistically.

The theory that your ultraconscious forces artificial misery on you is a bit more speculative than others in this book, but I mention it here because, if true, or arguably true, or partially true, it is supremely relevant to your happiness and crucial to explaining the oft-random and incomprehensible ups and downs of your life.

We can of course plan things we enjoy: travel, friends, lovers, a cup of coffee, a book, puzzles, food, kindness to a stranger – the list is endless on our planet, and your ultraconscious will permit their enjoyment, most of the time. But if something causes too much joy, he'll make sure it doesn't last long. Listen to your favorite song too many times and it won't be your favorite song anymore. A joke, novel, movie or place, no matter how much we enjoyed them at first, will grow stale. Even people can grow tiresome.

Observers long ago started noticing what has come to be known as the pleasure paradox, also known as the paradox of hedonism: happiness is best achieved only when it is not pursued. Go after it and you will fail.

"Those only are happy who have their minds fixed on some object other than their own happiness," wrote the philosopher John Stuart Mill in his 1873 *Autobiography*. "Ask yourself whether you are happy, and you cease to be so."

Or, as writer and politician William Bennett put it more recently, "Happiness is like a cat. If you try to coax it or call it, it will avoid you. It will never come. But if you pay no attention to it and go about your business, you'll find it rubbing up against your legs and jumping into your lap."

So what happens when you try to beat the ultraconscious at his own game, to tinker chemically with your brain to produce unearned joy? Those drugs that generate the shortest path to a sensation your conscious interprets as happiness – alcohol, hallucinogens, and powerful stimulants like cocaine – often produce the most severe rebound effects, such as depression and hangover. And, with serious overuse, they can lead to catastrophic ruin: bankruptcy, divorce, job loss, and health and psychological problems. These outcomes can most often be attributed to the physical and mental degradation that result from drug abuse, but – knowing what we do about the ultraconscious – we might also see his hand in the works, stomping among the gears and levers of your conscious existence, inflicting severe pain every time you presume to appropriate a pleasure for yourself you haven't earned and he hasn't approved.

Nor can wealth secure dependable happiness, it seems. According to numerous studies reviewed by psychologist Tim Kasser in *The High Price of Materialism*, those who focus their lives on the accumulation of money and things – even if these pursuits are successful – report a higher incidence of depression than less materialistic people.[40] In *Happiness: Lessons From a New Science*, Richard Layard writes of a "happiness syndrome" which forces us onto an endless "hedonic treadmill" of increasing acquisition to maintain the same level of happiness. Writes Layard, ". . . living standards are to some extent like alcohol or drugs (where) you need to keep on having more of it if you want to sustain your happiness."[41]

Focusing on the inability of material possessions to deliver happiness, Marsha L. Richins describes a post-purchase "hedonic decline," particularly among "high-materialism consumers." Ironically, these are the consumers most committed to happiness through shopping, but any happiness they feel before buying yields to sorrow afterwards.[42]

You can't demand happiness or force it on yourself with drugs or acquisition, and the reasons seem to lie deep within the human psyche, with the way our brains have been programmed.

I could dedicate a whole book to the countless lives broken on the rocks of joyous success and grand acquisition, but I hope a few case studies will – if they don't prove the ideas of this section – at least rouse your suspicions. There are distinct patterns of agony that occur in successful people's lives. Perhaps they have happened in your life, or someone you know or a famous person not mentioned here (the gossip tabloids are full of these stories). My aim is not to present so many stories that this gets tiresome, but to share enough anecdotes and statistics to suggest consistency. So let's turn now to some of the victims of happiness, and invite them to tell us in their own words how painful ecstasy can be:

M. Scott Peck. Born in 1936, M. Scott Peck was a psychologist who, as he practiced, began composing a philosophy of life and spirituality that he wrapped up in a book entitled *The Road Less Traveled*. The book, published in 1978, received little attention at first, but Peck was determined to see his ideas succeed and he promoted the work through extensive traveling and speaking.

Unfortunately for his mental health, Peck's efforts paid off, and as he neared his 50th birthday in the early 1980s, he arrived at a new place of joy. He had money, fame and, he admits, plenty of extramarital sex. In his 1997 book *In Search of Stones*, Peck recalled his life as a popular speaker, receiving "substantial lecture fees" as he dallied about the nation.

Simultaneously, Peck notes, the beauty of nature "was no longer the turn-on it had once been . . . great meals also ceased to be a turn-on . . . In short order, great art similarly became unimportant."[43] And then, he wrote:

> By 1984, my increasing fame had shifted from being an excitement to a burden. It felt like a trap. And soon even beautiful women stopped looking so glamorous. Along about this time I began to feel depressed. It's hard to put one foot in front of another when nothing turns you on anymore.[44]

Fame is the holy grail of human existence. If you are famous, you can go anywhere, do anything and always find people who want to be your friends and lovers. They will tell you how much they admire your work, how much they admire *you*. If you need something – money, sex, a job or a ride to the next town – you can get it wherever you go when you are famous (or infamous – the notorious John Dillinger received numerous marriage proposals while in jail).

So perhaps Peck's ultraconscious, observing from deep within the gray folds of Peck's brain that extraordinary happiness was disrupting Peck's evolved and carefully maintained emotional balance, launched a counterattack. Peck didn't describe the process as an ultraconscious attack, of course. He comes across as mystified by the whole affair. But in his words we can detect the iron fist of the cruel being who lurks behind the curtain of every human conscious:

> In the autumn of 1986 it felt like I was dying. Not physically dying – that I would have welcomed. It felt more like being in the Garden on the eve of my crucifixion, except that's an exaggeration. I wasn't sweating blood. I was, however, frightened and tearful.[45]

In the midst of his pain, Peck took up the violin, seriously considering a departure from the book-writing field for a move to concert musician. Which brings us to our next case.

Bernard Taupin. One of the most successful songwriters of all time, Bernard Taupin teamed up with Elton John to compose megahits like *Your Song, Bennie And The Jets, Daniel, Goodbye Yellow Brick Road,* and *Rocket Man.*

The success was devastating. From the June 23, 1980 *People* magazine.

> For 13 years Bernie Taupin had been Elton John's lyricist and thus one-half of Britain's most celebrated songwriting team since Lennon & McCartney. But after sharing in the glory with Captain Fantastic (Bernie toured with Elton and was occasionally dragged onstage) — not to mention the profits from an incredible 100 million sales — Taupin went into an emotional tailspin. "We'd filled the biggest stadiums and sold the most records," he explains. "Once we started acquiring palatial mansions, the meaning went out of rock 'n' roll." Hits came so easily that he and Elton dashed off one whole album in 10 days and, says Bernie, "There was nothing to do the rest of the year. I was bored and depressed." After two straight LPs entered the Billboard charts at No. 1 (a feat unequaled), Taupin began to wonder, "Where do we go from here?" So when their 1977 Blue Moves LP hit the charts "only" at No. 3, "We thought we were finished," he reports. Bernie was 27. That proved to be his last complete LP with Elton. Meanwhile Taupin's other partnership, a five-year marriage to Maxine Fiebelman, had also broken up. "I had no straws left to grab onto," he remembers. "So I turned to the bottle." His bender lasted two months before a shaken Taupin "mellowed out and dried out" in Acapulco. He also swore off music: "I figured that rock 'n' roll had destroyed me."[46]

Again, we see key elements of ultraconscious provocation, particularly fame and vast wealth. While Peck's ultraconscious wielded primarily the torment of spontaneous depression, Taupin's sorrow seems to have had both external and internal causes. Along with the parting of ways with Elton John and the end of his marriage, we see suffering that might owe its roots to the internal demons of the ultraconscious: alcohol abuse and professional self-doubt and disappointment following the lesser performance of *Blue Moves* (some people spend all their lives trying to get an album in the top 20; being sad about coming in at number 3 says a great deal about the brain's ability to set its own agenda for what makes us happy and what makes us sad).

Taupin and Peck both sought to flee from the source of their success, Taupin away from music, Peck to it. The pain was obviously neither music nor successful authorship, but something deeper: success, we might speculate.

Modern music is littered with the corpses of successful, ruined people – Janice Joplin, Jimi Hendrix, Kurt Cobain, Jim Morrison, Keith Moon, Elvis Presley, Amy Winehouse, Whitney Houston – who took their lives one way or another. We must wonder if the oft-sudden wealth and fame that comes particularly to popular musicians triggers such a backlash of ultraconscious misery that death sometimes becomes almost inevitable, either through suicide or the abuse of psychoactives (alcohol, hallucinogens etc.), the only thing strong enough to dull the sharp knives of the heartless ultraconscious.

And what of that other field that grants too much fame and wealth at too young an age? Was it, ultimately, the ultraconscious that killed actors and actresses James Dean, Marilyn Monroe, River Phoenix, Heath Ledger, Judy Garland?

The King of Ecclesiastes. The misery that follows success is an ancient story. Sometime before 250 BC, a wise and wealthy man, possibly Israel's King Solomon, wrote of his experiences with achievement and depression in verse that was eventually added to the Old Testament canon under the title Ecclesiastes.

The writer first describes a happy, successful existence:

I undertook great projects: I built houses for myself
and planted vineyards. I made gardens and parks and

planted all kinds of fruit trees in them. I made reservoirs to water groves of flourishing trees. I bought male and female slaves and had other slaves who were born in my house. I also owned more herds and flocks than anyone in Jerusalem before me. I amassed silver and gold for myself, and the treasure of kings and provinces. I acquired men and women singers, and a harem as well — the delights of the heart of man. I became greater by far than anyone in Jerusalem before me. In all this my wisdom stayed with me. I denied myself nothing my eyes desired; I refused my heart no pleasure. My heart took delight in all my work, and this was the reward for all my labor. (Ecclesiastes 2: 4-10)

But then, as with Bernie Taupin and M. Scott Peck, who would come long after him, depression hits our wealthy poet:

Yet when I surveyed all that my hands had done, and what I had toiled to achieve, everything was meaningless, a chasing after the wind; nothing was gained under the sun. . . . So I hated life, because the work that is done under the sun was grievous to me. . . . I hated all the things I had toiled for under the sun, because I must leave them to the one who comes after me. . . . So my heart began to despair over all my toilsome labor under the sun (excerpted from Ecclesiastes 2: 11-20).

A similar sentiment has been attributed to Abd Er-Rahman III, who ruled in the area that became Spain in the 10th century AD:

I have now reigned about 50 years in victory or peace, beloved by my subjects, dreaded by my enemies, and respected by my allies. Riches and honors, power and pleasure, have waited on my call, nor does any earthly blessing appear to have been wanting to my felicity. In this situation, I have diligently numbered the days of pure and genuine

happiness which have fallen to my lot. They amount
to fourteen.

Wealth, power, sex – and then sorrow. What a dilemma is
human existence. Fire, the wheel, and the futility of happiness
through acquisition all were discovered long ago. Fortunately for
human progress, only the third of these has been forgotten and
ignored, over and over again.

The Lottery Winner's Curse. Not everyone who wins the
lottery is destroyed by it. But winning the lottery does little for long
term happiness[47], and there have been enough spectacular failures
that the "lottery winner's curse" has entered common usage. Of the
catastrophes, how many were engineered by the ultraconscious to
balance the joy of riches? Here are a few of the most noteworthy
stories on that score, summarized by freelance writer Sherri Granato
in 2006:

> William "Bud" Post won $16.2 million in the
> Pennsylvania lottery in 1988 but now lives on his
> $450.00 a month Social Security check after relatives,
> and an ex-girlfriend tormented him until he invested
> and shared his millions with them.

> The 2002, $314.9 million dollar Powerball winner
> Jack Whittaker was sued by an Atlantic City casino in
> 2004 for allegedly writing bad checks from a closed
> bank account in West Virginia.

> Evelyn Adams, who won the $5.4 million dollar New
> Jersey lottery not just once, but twice in 1985 and
> again in 1986 gambled most of it away, and is broke
> today.

> 1993 Missouri lottery winner Janite Lee won $18
> million, but was overly generous by giving the money
> away to a variety of causes leading to her filing
> bankruptcy just eight years after her stroke of good
> fortune hit.

Billie Bob Harrell Jr. hit the $37 million dollar Texas jackpot in 1997 only to end his own life less than two years later when he realized that he wanted his marriage more than the money, but that it was too late to fix the strained marriage. Why was it strained? His spending habits spiraled out of control, and his wife only wanted a normal life which was anything but.[48]

Postpartum Depression. Given that the rules of evolution favor those most inclined toward reproduction, it's no surprise most women are powerfully driven to have children. And, given that there may be a correlation between the achievement of one's dreams and ensuing sorrow, it makes sense perhaps that for a significant number of women, childbirth is followed by depression.

Anywhere from 5 to 25 percent of new mothers suffer from postpartum depression, depending on the study, and because most do not respond to antidepressants, one might guess that the problem runs deeper than a change in hormones or other chemicals. While the incidence of postpartum depression seems to correlate with many other stress factors, ranging from self-esteem issues and lack of spousal support to cigarette smoking and a past history of depression, we might sometimes find the ultimate cause to be the ultraconscious, answering the new mother's happiness with cruel strokes of sorrow.

Paternal postpartum depression also exists and steals the happiness of a comparable number of new fathers, anywhere from 4 to 25 percent.[49 and 50]

The Malady of Modern Civilization. Now, what of large groups who achieve happiness en masse? More specifically, will the modern world, with its conveniences, its pain relievers and its unprecedented freedom from fear and want, provoke a backlash among the ultraconsciouses of some percentage of the newly-blessed populace?

"Worldwide," observed the World Health Organization in 2008, "suicide rates have increased by 60 percent over the last 50 years, and the increase has been particularly marked in developing countries."[51]

A large study of mental illness trends among American high school and college students suggests that depression has risen considerably from the difficult years of the 1930s to the far easier first years of the 21st century.

Jean Twenge and her fellow researchers looked at the scores of almost 80,000 students who took the Minnesota Multiphasic Personality Inventory, or MMPI, from 1938 to 2007, and discovered a marked increase in many areas of mental illness:

> Compared to college students in the 1930s and 1940s, recent U.S. college students score more than a standard deviation higher on the F scale (a measure of unusual responses), Psychopathic Deviation, Paranoia, Schizophrenia, and Hypomania, more than three-fourths of an SD higher on Hypochondrasis, Depression, Psychasthenia, and .45 SDs higher on Hysteria.[52]

In layman's terms, these findings indicate an increase across the board in mental distress, including a 600 percent increase in depression, from 1 percent of respondents to 6 percent. The number might be even higher, the study noted: "Given that increasing numbers of Americans are taking antidepressants, this data may actually underestimate the increase in psychopathology, as the samples from more recent years probably included more individuals already stabilized by SSRIs and other psychotropic medications."

The researchers considered a variety of possible causes of this phenomenon and propose that at least part of the blame may be placed on "an increased focus on money, appearance, and status rather than on community and close relationships." Similar conclusions were reached by Randolph Nesse and George Williams, who theorized that modern conditions like the absence of strong kin relationships and constant media portrayals of more attractive people make us sad.[53] But one can't help wondering if we might also find the ultraconscious lurking behind this data, stabbing more and more of us with pain because the natural world no longer inflicts enough of it.

Now, another point to ponder: If pain is truly so important to the ultraconscious that it must inflict it artificially, might he sometimes get us to inflict it upon ourselves?

Assisting Your Ultraconscious Through Self-Balancing

Self-torment is a common practice among humans, and one might wonder if the ultraconscious is once again to blame; the infliction of pain on oneself has a long, colorful and mostly religious history.

Devotees of many faiths over the centuries have imposed a wide array of discomfort on their bodies, from sleep deprivation and extreme hunger (fasting is a central element of various religions observations, including Christian Lent and Muslim Ramadan), to the use of unpleasant garments (hair shirts, sack cloth), to the employment of various, oft-torturous devices (the cilice, whips, skewers, flays, rods etc.).

Wrote Paul to the Corinthians, "No, I beat my body and make it my slave so that after I have preached to others, I myself will not be disqualified for the prize." (I Corinthians 9:27)

"Lord, either let me suffer or let me die," prayed St. Teresa of Ávila in the 16th century.

"(S)uffering is the process through which we mature," said Pope Benedict XVI in 2000 (while he was still a cardinal). "Anyone who has inwardly accepted suffering becomes more mature and more understanding of others, becomes more human."[54]

Benedict's immediate predecessor, Pope John Paul, reportedly performed regular self-flagellation with a belt. "As some members of his closest entourage were able to hear with their own ears, Karol Wojtyla flagellated himself both in Poland and in the Vatican," wrote Msgr. Slawomir Oder, in a 2010 book that presents the evidence in favor of the pope's beatification. "In his closet, among the cassocks, there was a hook holding a particular belt for slacks, which he used as a whip. . ."[55]

Demonstrations of primitive mysticism make we moderns uneasy. Whirling dervishes, shouting prophets, entranced voodoo priestesses and men pushing metal pins through their cheeks are similarly unwelcome in the public sphere, the modern workplace and at most dinner parties.

But the mortifiers of flesh have not vanished. They have either gone underground, suffering in private, or have found new names and logical justifications for their self torment. Gyms, tracks and roadsides throughout the modern world feature a grimacing, panting citizenry who have found that better health is the perfect excuse for a little anguish. Some wear t-shirts that celebrate, not the fitness that is the alleged goal of self-torment, but the suffering itself. "Pain is weakness leaving the body," reads one shirt I've seen during my own time at the gym. "Painfully addicted to iron," reads another. Search the internet with the phrase "pain gym t-shirt" and you'll find many more: "Train beyond the pain," "Bring the pain," and a whole line of t-shirts for a gym in Bournemouth, UK called House of Pain. No one bothers wearing "No pain no gain" t-shirts anymore. The saying is too cliché to be fashionable.

Another example of self-imposed unpleasantness, from the business world:

> One of (our) top franchisees – who sells more than a million dollars of products and services every year – does, in fact, get up before dawn every day to take a cold shower. Why? He says he does it because a cold shower wakes him up! However, he also says the cold shower is symbolic of winning. He could "wimp out," he explains, and take a comfortable, hot shower, or he could immediately jump in the "winner's circle" by taking a cold shower.[56]

Call it winning or exercise or good health or spiritual discipline. These may be what your ultraconscious wants you to think you're doing. But this chapter proposes that much of our pain is no more than pain for pain's sake, sown and reaped by your ultraconscious in the same way humans plant and harvest wheat. The crops, of discomfort, sorrow, memory, are brought in regularly to keep you balanced, to keep you on the straight and narrow path of survival and reproduction, to ensure you always feel fully the next pain or pleasure.

Perhaps the Buddhists, the stoics and the self-flagellants have been right all along. Each has found ways to limit their happiness – through mechanical devices or some form of physical or emotional self-control – and thus to limit or at least channel the pain that accompanies happiness. One wonders if there might be a way to fool the ultraconscious into thinking you have suffered more than you actually have, in order to reap a bit more compensatory pleasure from your ultraconscious. Perhaps that's part of the reason acupuncture and deep tissue massage are helpful for some: they don't hurt as much as your brain thinks they do.

Now, what about the corollary? Is there any evidence that your ultraconscious offers artificial pleasure when you are suffering too much?

The Ultraconscious of Mercy

No matter what happens to us, it seems, we can bounce back. It might be merely the passage of time that lessens the sting, or it might be one of the many interesting psychological phenomena science has discovered. The reduction in pain, though, like the initial pain itself, isn't something we choose consciously. For the same reasons that the ultraconscious might be inflicting pain, he could also be relieving it. Following is some of the evidence for his more compassionate side.

In her book, *On Death and Dying,* Elizabeth Kubler-Ross identifies five states of grief that follow devastating news – the loss of a loved one, for example, or a report from the doctor about impending death. The first stage is denial, followed by anger, bargaining (in which one promises to do something different to make the problem go away), depression/apathy, and finally, acceptance, a stage marked by peace and even the return of joy.[57]

Eventually, that which at one time was so horrible as to be unthinkable is accepted as the new normal, as if an elephant in the living room shrinks down over time to the size of bric-a-brac. From a 2005 article in *Time* magazine about the science of happiness:

> (Happiness researcher David) Lykken proposed the idea that each of us has a happiness set point much like our set point for body weight. No matter what happens in our life – good, bad, spectacular, horrific – we tend to return in short order to our set range . . . (A) substantial body of research documents our tendency to return to the norm. . . Even people who lose the use of their limbs to a devastating accident tend to bounce back, though perhaps not all the way to their base line. One study found that a week after the accident, the injured were severely angry and anxious, but after eight weeks "happiness was their

strongest emotion," says (psychologist and happiness researcher Edward) Diener. Psychologists call this adjustment to new circumstances adaptation. "Everyone is surprised by how happy paraplegics can be," says (Nobel prize winning psychologist Daniel) Kahneman. "The reason is that they are not paraplegic full time. They do other things. They enjoy their meals, their friends. They read the news. . ."[58]

Acute Stress Reaction. One of the most famous sufferers of this condition was Elisabeth of Bavaria, attacked in 1898 by an anarchist just before boarding a boat in Geneva, Switzerland. She had been stabbed in the heart but continued on her journey as if nothing was wrong, consciously unaware of any problem until just before she bled to death. Her last words were, "What happened to me?" Acute stress reaction can set in within moments of being severely injured or receiving shocking news. The victim goes into a daze, becoming disoriented and losing the ability to perceive or respond to the pain or horror.

Because such a phenomenon is common during torture, the officials of the Catholic Inquisition sometimes kept doctors on hand to revive those being interrogated.

Repressed memory. A condition that sometimes follows acute stress reaction, repressed memory is the inability to recall stressful or traumatic events. Research indicates that the memory is retained in the brain but is not accessible by the conscious, although conscious recollection may later occur, perhaps when the memory is not so painful.

Endorphins. This word, a combination of the Latin words endogenous and morphine, may be translated as "a morphine-like substance originating within the body." Endorphins are compounds produced by the pituitary gland and hypothalamus and are released during, among other events, strenuous exercise, pain and injury, and orgasm. Like opiates, they reduce pain and generate feelings of euphoria. The runner's high that rewards some athletes during an extreme workout may result from a flood of endorphins.

Superstition. Belief in a deity or deities who care about you, protect you, give you wealth and peace, and vanquish your foes can be a powerful source of hope, confidence and happiness, particularly when life is difficult.

Dissociative Identity Disorder. Also called multiple personality disorder, the condition occurs when at least two personalities regularly take charge of the individual. Many sufferers report severe sexual and physical trauma in childhood, and it is theorized multiple personalities develop to help the individual cope with intolerably painful memories.

Peck and the Parkinson's Woman. Now we'll revisit two of the cases described a few pages ago and present some interesting additional details that seem to suggest the workings of a merciful ultraconscious. In Peck's case, temporary relief came in the form of what he called a spirit. In the case of the woman with Parkinson's, she seemed to receive a powerful, compensatory emotional boost as soon as her ordeal with the misplaced electrode was over.

Peck was suffering through the depths of his depression one evening in 1986 when he turned out the light to go to sleep. Immediately, he was "accosted by a good spirit and . . . it was entirely up to me whether I was going to let it in." Peck decided he was being visited by a "Spirit of Mirth," let it into his mind and "giggled myself to sleep.

"For the next two days I experienced some surcease from my depression. Thereafter I was depressed as usual until I came out of it about nine months later."[59]

In the case of the woman with Parkinson's, Damasio suggests, her mood became unusually elevated a few minutes after the electrode was turned off. "The sadness vanished from the patient's face . . . Very rapidly, she smiled, appeared relaxed, and for the next five minutes was quite playful, even jocular."[60]

How Understanding Secret 2 Might Make you Happier

If you have found this chapter understandable and believable, ideas for approaching life have probably rolled naturally off these pages. But, by way of review, here are a few ideas for pursuing and protecting your happiness:

1. Because huge improvements to your happiness may result in huge ultraconscious counteroffensives, pursue instead steady, incremental improvements.

Follow the example of deep sea divers who, after significant time underwater, must come up slowly or suffer the bends. Seek to win promotions, not lotteries. Rise slowly to the next joy, or the resulting pain may be unbearable, even fatal.

2. Know that when something awful happens, happiness will still be possible, even inevitable. As you suffer, you will find solace in things you never noticed before, and you will find strange moments of pleasure. Let them come.

3. No matter what you achieve, no matter the heights of your wealth, fame, success, love or happiness, pain will be a regular visitor. Contrarily, even if your life is completely ordinary, you have very likely experienced the same degree of joy and suffering as the wealthiest, the most famous, the most beautiful and loved among us. We humans have had to do many, many things to win the fight of evolution, and pain and pleasure have long been the principal tools directing these behaviors. Pleasure and pain may be like blood and bone, central to your composition, inescapable parts of everything you are. Enjoy the former, endure the latter. No matter who you are, this is quite likely your inescapable lot in life.

4. Human technology will continue to enable greater happiness and less pain. Avail yourself of it. Surgical anesthesia, pain killers, anti-depressants, all have their place, and a great deal of excellent research is being done on non-chemical paths to greater happiness – exercises in developing a more positive outlook, combating your negative thoughts, formally expressing gratitude, letting your pain spur you on to action. Earlier in this chapter, I mentioned Aaron Beck, who discovered that his depressed patients would torment themselves with "automatic thoughts." Beck taught his patients to counteract these thoughts consciously, by fighting them with logic.

Do any additional lessons emerge from the stories told earlier in this chapter? I believe so.

The Kings in the Dark Nights. M. Scott Peck, when suffering the depths of his depression, met with a nun who told him he was experiencing the "dark night of the senses." He recalled this conversation with her:

> "Now what do I do about it?"
>
> "Nothing."
>
> *"Nothing?"*
>
> "Yes, nothing, she answered emphatically. "I can't tell you anything to do. I can only warn you what not to do. That is to try to go back, which some people do by seeking after ever more beautiful women or greater art."
>
> That made sense to me. "What do I do to go forward?" I asked.
>
> "Nothing. Just wait."
>
> "Wait? How long?"
>
> "I have no idea," she replied. "Eventually, you'll come out the other side. It won't be the same as it was. It will feel better that it is now. But not as it was. It will be different, but I can't tell you how long it will take."[61]

Peck continued to suffer for another 18 months before his ordeal finally ended. He wrote:

> "When it lifted, it was not like it was before. Before my joy had been the product of external events: a new romance, a new book, a great review, a dramatic stride forward by the foundation with which we worked, an accomplishment of a child. Now my joy, while hardly constant, was purely internal and unrelated to circumstances. Success didn't seem to do much to lift me up, and failure didn't bring me down. Some days, when my life seemed to be going badly and people asked, "How are you doing, Scotty?" I'd answer, "Great, although I've got no idea why."[62]

Perhaps we can solve Peck's riddle.

As they journeyed together over the hard road of his fame and resulting depression, Peck and his ultraconscious finally came to terms, and he was at last restored to a stable program of emotional balance. Going forward, he would no longer be allowed to enjoy the happiness of his achievements, since they were coming too thick and fast for his ultraconscious to counter without extreme, life-threatening attacks. So Peck would be permitted contentment, but only within the new confines the ultraconscious had worked out for him.

And what of our Biblical sufferer, the author of Ecclesiastes? After he had enjoyed his wealth and success, and then suffered the despair that seems invariably to follow joy, he reached a place not too different from Peck's: "A man can do nothing better than to eat and drink and find satisfaction in his work," our king observed in Ecclesiastes 2:24.

As for Bernard Taupin, in 1993 he traded in the "palatial mansions" of his earlier life to satisfy a "boyhood dream" with the purchase of "a modest ranch in the Santa Ynez Valley" where he was still living in 2011, according to his website.[63] The website suggests that Taupin, like Peck and the king in Ecclesiastes, found meaning in the simple pleasures of life. His website biography (authored by his wife, Heather) refers to him several times with the humble title "brown dirt cowboy" and notes that he is an "avid reader" who consumes "over 40 books annually, ranging from the classics and American history to biographies of jazz, blues and country pioneers; it is by far his favorite relaxation method." Adds the narrative, "He is also an exceptional cook and loves to host his closest friends and family . . . the brown dirt cowboy's barbecue sauce is blue ribbon worthy."

The idea behind these closing narratives, which might constitute a fifth principle to be added to the four from earlier in this section, can be summed up this way: Never lose the ability to enjoy the simple things, the small pleasures, the food and people of your world. These were the stuff of happiness for eons as we evolved, so, most likely, our happiness is still inescapably bound to them. Forgetting them in the pursuit of palaces, fame and success, even if such pursuits are successful – indeed, especially if they are successful – can be a recipe for emotional disaster.

In Conclusion: Other Powers of the Ultraconscious

We have leveled some serious charges so far against the insidious half of your brain. He works secretly to write the story of your existence, both the good and the bad. Following an ancient template evolved in a very different world, he decides what pain and pleasures you feel, manufacturing both from whole cloth when he can't find them in the larger world around you. He holds in his cruel, ancient hands much of the enjoyment you are able to eke out in your life.

Obviously, a system that can calibrate your very enjoyment of life must hold tremendous powers over many other elements of your existence, what you feel physically, what your senses tell you, and even how you reason.

Indeed.

Secret 3: Your Ultraconscious is a Liar

You are, to put it bluntly, in a very intimate, very difficult relationship with a highly controlling individual you can't get rid of who doesn't want what you want.

Fortunately, you, the conscious part of your existence, have plenty of power in this relationship. You hold ultimate authority over what you do and say, where you go, what you think about. For whatever reason, evolution long ago granted the conscious this power. Unlike simpler animals, whose behavior is strictly the autonomic response to stimuli, your conscious can question, it can doubt, it can say, "Stop, wait, I'm not sure I want to do this."

The jury's still out on why evolution would favor creatures with a conscious, a part of the brain separate and independent from the ultraconscious. Perhaps advanced animals needed a conscious to solve new problems in a varied environment, or to mediate among the conflicting inclinations of the ultraconscious when he couldn't decide what to do. Perhaps verbal communication, so critical to the success of the human species, was impossible without a conscious.

Left to its own devices, of course, the conscious is an evolutionary failure. It might be good at day-to-day management, problem-solving and conversation, but it has no idea how the world works. Until it's explicitly told, your conscious doesn't know what's poisonous or safe to eat. It has to learn, through trial and error, many of the rules for interacting with other people. It even has to be told that sex leads to babies!

So it's fine if the conscious sticks to its job description, but it must be kept on a short leash. Let the conscious stray and the result is certain: a short, childless existence.

What key ultraconscious tool evolved to keep the conscious in check? The answer, in one word: lies.

Yes, the most significant of your significant others isn't being honest with you. He is operating an extensive program of deception that makes you see things that aren't there, feel things that never happened and believe things that just ain't so.

The lies of the ultraconscious will be addressed in this and the next chapter. In the second of these chapters, I will cover the special category of lies known as superstition. In this chapter, I will present the considerable evidence that we are designed not to know. Instead, we are supposed to believe what we think we're seeing and what we think makes sense, because in the ancient world where we evolved, this was a good thing. In the modern world, of course, such an approach is woefully obsolete.

The secret discussed in this chapter may be captured with three simple, increasingly terrifying statements:

1.   Evolution favored reproductive winners – not the honest, not the seekers of truth and justice, not the kind, generous or self-aware – just the winners

2.   As the descendant of a long line of evolutionary winners, you have inherited their nature

3.   So has everyone else

The Evolutionary Theory of Self-Deception

Your ultraconscious, like a dictator or an abusive spouse, uses rewards and punishments to control you, but he has also evolved an elaborate, efficient system of delusion, hiding the truth from you and creating lies for your consumption with equal ease.

"Self-deception appears to be a universal human trait which touches our lives at all levels,"[64] writes Robert Trivers. "An evolutionary theory of self-deception – the active misrepresentation of reality to the conscious mind – suggests that there may be multiple sources of self-deception in our own species."[65]

Writing for a general audience, Shankar Vedantam is sympathetic to the challenges of wrapping our minds around this twisted reality:

If you now feel as I once did when I first began learning about these ideas, you might . . . be a little offended that anyone would say you have a very limited understanding of what is happening in your own head, that the feeling of "common sense" we all experience is an illusion no less fake – and far more spectacular – than the sun's daily journey across the sky.[66]

And yet, the evidence of our self-delusion is overwhelming and continues to grow. The lies described in this chapter are organized under three categories:

Physical lies
Cognitive lies
Emotional lies

Physical Lies

We, our conscious selves, are being constantly fooled by our brains to ensure optimal reproductive behaviors. Following are a few examples:

Cryptic Ovulation. Animals know when they are ovulating, and their minds have evolved to make sure they do the right things at that most critical time. The male animal mind has evolved in partnership with the female, so that he knows when the female is ready and pursues her with absolute determination. Chemical signals, changes in color, new behaviors and sounds, all are used by female animals to get the point across.

Except for humans. We are surely the only species on earth that has identified the connection between the sex act and offspring. And, because giving birth and raising children are difficult, we are likely the only species who ever refrained from sex to avoid pregnancy. Of course, avoiding pregnancy is exactly the wrong thing to do from the perspectives of evolutionary success, or of what your ultraconscious wants. So something new would have to evolve to counter human intelligence before we thought ourselves into oblivion.

Imagine two ancient tribes, both blessed with an awareness of the connection between intercourse and birth. The females of

Tribe 1 ovulate quite obviously, and they avoid dalliances at those times to save themselves trouble. Only when a particular woman wants a child will she mate during ovulation, but those times are rare. Children are difficult enough in the modern world, with its cribs and diapers, day care and doctors. No one wants to give birth on a camping trip, and life was one big camping trip back then.

Now, in Tribe 2, there's been a bizarre mutation. The women don't know when they're fertile. Signs are hidden, or indecipherable, to both the women and the men (not that the men's awareness is that important, men always being ready for sex). In Tribe 1, babies are conceived only when the women want them. In Tribe 2, conception is often unintended – and far more frequent.

Predictably, Tribe 1 fades away, and Tribe 2 gives birth to us all, thanks to what scientists call cryptic ovulation.

"(N)atural selection concealed homind ovulation to counter a human or prehuman conscious tendency among females," hypothesized anthropologist Nancy Burley in 1979, "to avoid conception through abstinence from intercourse near ovulation."[67]

Obviously, conscious ignorance of ovulation isn't the only thing evolution has devised to get people to make babies. The female's ultraconscious knows when she is ovulating, and women tend to be more sexually active at those times, according to a significant amount of research. Men's ultraconsciouses probably also know. One study of 18 exotic dancers found that the tips they earned for lap dances almost doubled while they were ovulating.[68]

The ultimate reason humans don't know when ovulation is taking place remains unknown, and it has also been proposed that cryptic ovulation ensures that sex can occur throughout the woman's cycle, ensuring closer bonds and a stronger relationship for child-rearing.

Regardless the reason, the phenomenon is remarkable, especially in that it occurs in the planet's most intelligent species. The ultraconscious doesn't say anything explicit to the woman's conscious about her reproductive state, and the physical cues have been subdued as well, keeping her and the males around her in the dark (consciously, at least) about her vulnerability to what is surely one of the most momentous physical conditions of her life.

Pain is in the Brain. My uncle played college football in the days when they didn't wear much protective padding. In one game, after a series of rough plays, the ball changed hands and he and his teammates left the field. As my uncle met with his coach on the sidelines, he swatted at something on his shoulder but barely noticed it for several minutes.

Finally, he looked at the source of the irritation and noticed that his collar bone had snapped in two.

This isn't a story about how tough my uncle was. Toughness alone doesn't explain his ignorance of a serious injury. In fact, he didn't feel the injury because, most likely, *his ultraconscious didn't want him to.*

Athletes in intense competition, soldiers in combat and others in emergency situations often report the absence of pain despite grievous injuries.

Why? The answer becomes obvious if we imagine things from the perspective of your lying ultraconscious. While you're in a life and death fight, or playing a violent game of football that might feel to your ultraconscious like mortal combat, pain is a dangerous, potentially deadly distraction. Pain has some important benefits, but it is most beneficial if it can be controlled without conscious input.

The amount of pain you feel is not equal to the amount of damage your body has suffered. Pain reaches your conscious only after it has been cleared to do so by your ultraconscious, in the quantity he prescribes.

The idea that pain is more a mental than a physical phenomenon was first put forth in the 1960s by Canadian psychologist Ronald Melzack and British physician Patrick David Wall. In an article published in *Science* in 1965,[69] Melzack and Wall proposed the gate control theory of pain, which revolutionized the understanding and treatment of pain (and led to a new generation of pain-killing drugs). They have described the theory as outlining "a more dynamic conception in which pain is determined by many factors in addition to injury – by past experiences, culture, attention, and other activities in the nervous system at the time of injury."[70]

Dreams. Anyone who has ever dreamed knows that the brain has a powerful capacity for creating alternative realities that your conscious finds very believable.

No one is certain what dreams are for. I would guess they serve a variety of survival and reproductive functions, and speculation has taken many fascinating turns. Researchers studying the brains of sleeping people, for example, have found they tend to fire in patterns that match the waking activities of the preceding day.

So let's imagine your ultraconscious is indeed the author of your dreams. What might he be up to?

Perhaps, depending on the dream's content, he wants you thinking about reproduction (sex dreams), or wants you exposed to sexual symbology (the train entering the tunnel), or preparing a plan if you're attacked (I suffer a recurring nightmare of being chased by someone who wants to kill me), or testing reproductive behaviors to see how your conscious will react (for example, public nudity, a dream that for most of us modern, modest humans results in a very clear message back to the ultraconscious that this is a bad idea).

Dreams may also be a way for the ultraconscious to see what he can pull over on you. Most of the time, we wake up and quickly realize the dreams were just that, but people sometimes believe. As shall be proposed in the next chapter, the ultraconscious uses religion extensively to keep us on the path toward reproduction, and religious dreams can reinforce a person's superstitions, or even create them. I knew a non-religious woman who became a Christian because of a dream she had about God. She remained a believer long enough to go to church, meet a man there and marry him.

If we accept that your brain comes in two parts, conscious and ultraconscious, dreams are not consciously created and so must by our definition be produced by the ultraconscious, and they reveal impressive powers, not just to show you something that isn't real, but to make you believe that it *is* real.

Anorexia Nervosa. In this extreme form of physical self delusion, people become so obsessed with losing weight that they sometimes starve themselves to death. "In extreme cases," notes the Mayo Clinic website, sufferers "may be skeletally thin but still think they're fat."

Phantom Pain. There are times when we don't feel the pain that we should. There are other times when we do feel pain that we shouldn't.

The most obvious example of the latter is phantom limb pain, when a long-gone arm or leg continues to report not just its existence, but some painful distress – a burning sensation, the perpetual clenching of a muscle, or a persistent ache. Interestingly, such pain can sometimes be made to go away by tricking the ultraconscious. In one study, researchers, working with people who had phantom pain in a leg no longer there, set up a mirror next to the remaining leg so that it looked like the missing leg was back where it belonged. Some patients reported relief after simply looking at the two limbs, even though one was an illusion.[71]

Of course, all of us, whether intact or not, have experienced unexplainable pain. Headaches, stomach distress, backache, a sudden twinge in a joint, are often just as strange as the pain of a missing arm. Pain may have value in keeping us from damaging our bodies, but what use is a spontaneous spasm in the calf, or a migraine? I suffer migraines a few times a month and a bad episode hurts so much I can only lie in the dark until it passes. How does that further my ultraconscious's reproductive aims?

Pain, it seems, is managed and carefully applied by the same ultraconscious that makes up our dreams and our many other delusions.

Placebos for Pain. It is generally accepted that a statistically significant number of people are cured by placebos – fake medicines, sham surgeries, bogus procedures and such.

The belief in placebos is so widespread that almost half of doctors in the US surveyed for a 2008 study admitted to prescribing various substances, including over-the-counter painkillers, vitamins, sedatives and antibiotics, with no known relevance to the patient's complaint.[72]

Testing of new medications often includes some percentage of test subjects who receive only placebos, and the treatment will be called a failure if the placebo group gets better at the same rate as those taking the actual medication. Recovery in such cases is instead attributed to the mysterious placebo effect, in which the illusion of a cure produces a cure.

The underlying assumption here is fascinating: Some force, which we may safely theorize is the ultraconscious, knows you are taking a pill and sometimes chooses to make you better because of it, even if the pill is made of sugar.

It's a fascinating possibility, but quite possibly false under all but one interesting condition.

In a study published in 2001 in *The New England Journal of Medicine,* Asbjorn Hrobjartsson and Peter C. Gotzsche looked at more than 100 clinical studies of various drugs and treatments and found no clear evidence of a placebo effect in any of them except those in which pain was being treated.[73] Studies of placebo effects on a wide variety of pain – back pain, breast pain, knee pain, post-operative pain, the pain of an intravenous needle – typically showed pain reductions regardless what the patient was being given.

"In 27 trials involving the treatment of pain, placebo had a beneficial effect, as indicated by a reduction in the intensity of pain," the authors wrote.

So, take a pain pill, or a sugar pill disguised as a pain pill, and it apparently fools your ultraconscious into loosening the screws a bit. Your ultraconscious cannot make the cancer or the physical injury or the flu go away, but when it serves his agenda, he can control how the problem feels. Why would he relieve your pain just because you took a sugar pill? We can only speculate, but as was noted earlier, pain doesn't seem to be entirely at his discretion. Sometimes, conscious efforts to reduce pain, no matter how physiologically irrelevant, are nevertheless heeded.

False Positives. If you've ever been on a large ship at sea, you're familiar with the constant, subtle sensations of movement that come with ocean travel. The ship bobs and rocks as it plies the waves and changes speed and direction, creating enough stimuli that it sickens some people.

Your conscious knows what's going on – you're at sea – but your ultraconscious is confused. Journeys in great vessels are one of the many things the human ultraconscious hasn't adapted to yet, so he finds it inexplicable and calculates it as a threat to your survival.

Psychologist Michel Treisman has theorized that strange movements in the environment make the brain suspect you've been poisoned by a hallucinogen, such as a mushroom or rotten food.[74] Thus, the solution that evolved long ago is the vomiting reflex. Your ultraconscious wants whatever's in your body gone.

The sensation of unexplainable rocking is so disconcerting to our primal systems that, for weeks after a cruise, many people continue to experience the sensation, a phenomenon known as "mal de debarquement." Doctors will tell their patients to keep taking motion sickness medications a week or more after they travel by sea. For my wife and me, our world continued to bob and sway for almost a month after sea travel, particularly in the shower or in other places where water was present. It was our ultraconsciouses, still worried about that odd sensation and saying, "Hey, I think whatever was going on earlier this month might be happening again. Did you just do whatever it was you did before?"

Post cruise dizziness is one of those examples where your ultraconscious senses something happening in the modern world that he has no evolved explanation for, it frightens him, and he goes on alert for reoccurrences, looking for any shred of evidence of a relapse. It's okay if it's wrong – if there's a false positive. If you didn't just eat a hallucinogen, no problem, the feeling will go away. But if there's the remotest chance you did just eat another hallucinogen, your ultraconscious wants you to know, and he'll duplicate the earlier sensations to the best of his ability so, first, he'll have your attention and, second, you'll know the specific threat he's trying to warn you about.

I've had a similar experience with my cell phone. I wear it on my hip and usually set it to vibrate. I'm not sure if my ultraconscious knows what that thing is, but I suspect he believes there's something wrong with my digestive system. Soon after I started wearing my phone that way, I would get the distinct sense of vibration on the right side of my stomach, even when no one was calling me.

We see faces and people in random textures or arrangements of trash. We hear voices in the wind. We feel spiders crawling on us after we've broken a web. "Here's something I want you to see, hear, feel, or smell," the ultraconscious is telling us, "just in case it's real, since it was such bad news last time. Please check it out!"

This feature of the mind has particular value in life-and-death situations, especially war: "The guerrilla has good reason to see his enemy in every bush and hear him in every snapping twig," writes Stewart Guthrie. "One real enemy justifies a hundred false alarms."[75]

Cognitive Lies

Your ultraconscious stands accused by modern science of lying to you to get you to survive and reproduce without any regard for your happiness.

To this point, I have cited as evidence only those lies that involve your physical senses. Somewhere along the path from the physical event – injury, ovulation, a rocking boat – to your conscious perception of it, information is getting deleted or manipulated. In other instances – dreams, pain, dizziness – information is being fashioned from whole cloth by your ultraconscious.

But fooling your senses is just part of the ultraconscious agenda to keep you in the dark. He also inserts himself among the very gears of your conscious thinking, lying to you repeatedly about reality and what you believe are your own, completely rational thoughts.

The Thinker, Auguste Rodin's famed bronze and marble sculpture, is incomplete, for it shows only a single naked man sitting on a rock with his chin resting on his knuckles. To more accurately reflect conscious thought, Rodin should have cast a second figure, our ultraconscious, standing behind the thinker, his hands shoved deep into the thinker's skull, his busy fingers working constantly, invisibly.

Strategic Cognitive Self-Ignorance. We take for granted that we forget, make mistakes, and draw the wrong conclusions, but given the apparent power of our brains to store everything and perform countless operations per second, these weaknesses should make us wonder. Why would your super-intelligent ultraconscious allow you to forget an essential grocery item, an important person's name or a crucial step on the job?

We might theorize that you don't remember and don't get things right for the same reason you don't feel injuries and don't recognize ovulation – because your ultraconscious doesn't want you to.

Many times, the value of these mistakes are difficult to fathom. But evolutionary psychologists and behavioral scientists are uncovering a growing catalog of behaviors where people make exactly the right mistakes for ensuring reproductive success.

Research indicates that people are, for example, remarkably good at neglecting any information that weakens their case. Be it a legal dispute, a disagreement at work or an argument with a spouse, our profound capacity for logic and understanding is hijacked by the need to win, even if our victory harms another person unfairly.

As Robert Wright put it, "the human brain wants victory, not truth."[76]

A number of studies have shown that people will quickly forget facts that do not bolster their case, while they firmly retain helpful facts. According to the theory of fundamental attribution error,[77] you will blame someone else's bad behavior on their character, while you will excuse your own questionable actions on the particular circumstances that produced the behavior.

Research indicates that it's not just that you work consciously (and sneakily) to deceive your adversary, the judge or someone else observing the fight. The evidence suggests that to make the strongest presentation, *you yourself must also be deceived.*

In the foreword to the first edition of Richard Dawkin's *The Selfish Gene*, Robert L. Trivers became the first to formally articulate the concept that natural selection would favor the ability to lie to oneself without conscious awareness. "(I)f deceit is fundamental in animal communication," Trivers wrote, "then there must be strong selection to spot deception and this ought, in turn, to *select for a degree of self-deception, rendering some facts and motives unconscious* (my emphasis) so as not to betray – by the subtle signs of self knowledge – the deception being practiced."[78]

Wright described it this way: ". . . the aura of rightness surrounding so many of our actions may be delusional; even when they feel right, they may do harm."[79] He adds, "The human brain is, in large part, a machine for winning arguments, a machine for convincing others that its owner is in the right – and thus, *a machine for convincing its owner of the same thing.*"[80]

In 1998, Harvard anthropologist Richard Wrangham noted the many studies showing that people often believe they are more competent than they are, and proposed two theories for how such "positive illusions" might be helpful.

In Wrangham's Performance Enhancement Hypothesis, excessive self-confidence reduces stress, increases cohesion within groups and keeps performance-interfering doubt in check.

Wrangham's Opponent-Deception Hypothesis proposes that positive illusions, because they have fooled the person experiencing them, will fool the opponent and could lead the rival to back down before the fight or contest has even begun. "(I)n conflicts involving mutual assessment, an exaggerated assessment of the probability of winning increases the probability of winning," Wrangham wrote. "Selection therefore favors this form of overconfidence."[81]

Computer models have indicated the same thing, with one 2011 study concluding that "overconfidence maximizes individual fitness and . . . may help to explain why overconfidence remains prevalent today, even if it contributes to hubris, market bubbles, financial collapses, policy failures, disasters and costly wars."[82]

So what happens when you present people with overwhelming evidence that they are wrong? More specifically, what happens if you present mathematical data that supports a certain viewpoint someone finds objectionable? An experiment by Yale's Dan Kahan generated results both disappointing and quite predictable. Kahan and his fellow researchers showed test subjects data from the study of a highly-political topic, gun control, and found that "subjects (used) quantitative-reasoning capacity selectively to conform their interpretation of the data to the result most consistent with their political outlooks."[83]

Interestingly, the more numerically competent someone was, the more likely they would subvert that mathematical expertise to support their political opinion.

Speaking more generally about the value of self ignorance when working on a particular goal, David Buss writes, "nothing in evolutionary psychology requires that humans be aware of either the underlying psychological mechanisms or the ultimate function of goal pursuit."[84]

And as Trivers put it, ". . . the conventional view that natural selection favors nervous systems which produce ever more accurate images of the world must be a very naïve view of mental evolution."[85]

Trivers adds, "(W)hile it takes a nervous signal only about 20 milliseconds to reach the brain, it requires a full 500 milliseconds for a signal reaching the brain to register in consciousness! This is all the time in the world, so to speak, for emendations, changes, deletions, and enhancements to occur."[86]

In offering this assertion, Trivers cites the research of Benjamin Libet, who conducted extensive tests of the time it took for stimuli to be noticed by the conscious. Libet found that while an impulse would reach the brain and elicit a reflexive response in as little as 50 milliseconds (one millisecond equals one one-thousandth of a second, so 50 milliseconds equals one-twentieth of a second), the conscious awareness of the stimulus takes 500 milliseconds (half a second).[87] So, when you touch something, hear something, see something, the sensation reaches your brain almost instantly, but your conscious is kept in the dark for nearly half a second. What's going on during the gap? Trivers suggests that time is used creatively, by what we're calling the ultraconscious in this book, to make up things, to eliminate things, to package the stimulus in the way that best serves his purposes.

Ignorance is bliss, it has been said. Or, at least from the perspective of your ultraconscious, conscious ignorance is essential even if it is not exactly blissful.

Following are a few other examples of the ultraconscious' ability to fool your conscious, each remarkable in its own right, and each pointing to another facet of the human brain's powers of self-deception:

Split Brain Experiments. Treatments for severe epileptic seizures sometimes include severing the corpus callosum, the thick band of nerve cells that join the right and left halves, or hemispheres, of the brain.

People can survive and live normal lives without this connective band, but experiments have revealed the mental limitations of someone with a split brain, as well as hint at how the ultraconscious overcomes those limitations through effortless deceit.

In most people, the left brain handles logic, analysis, language, and other objective processing, while the right brain is more creative and subjective, taking a big picture approach to the questions of life. The left half of the brain also seems to be the place where most conscious processing takes place.

In most of us, these two halves of the brain are constantly checking with each other through the corpus callosum. But what happens if they can't?

Oddly enough, portions of each eye send information about what is seen to either the left or right half of the brain. So researchers, when studying the brain with the help of a split-brain subject, would show information only to the field of view that sends signals to one half of the brain.

In one experiment, the researchers would show a large picture and then four smaller pictures to one side of the subject's field of vision, thus sending the image to only one hemisphere of the subject's brain. Then they would ask the subject to point to the small picture that went with the larger picture. For example, a large picture of a snowstorm would be shown, followed by a rake, pickaxe, lawnmower and snow shovel. The correct answer was the shovel, and the subject would point to it using the left hand, which was under the control of the same, right hemisphere.

Quickly afterwards, the subject's left hemisphere would be shown a large picture of a chicken's foot and small pictures that included a chicken, toaster, apple and hammer.

The right hand, under the control of the left hemisphere, would point correctly to the chicken. It's a bit confusing, but this is where things got interesting. The researchers have flashed two sets of images in quick succession to the subject, who has just pointed to a shovel with the left hand and to a chicken with the right hand:

> Then we asked the patient why the left hand – or right hemisphere – was pointing to the shovel. Because only the left hemisphere retains the ability to talk, it answered. But because it could not know why the right hemisphere was doing what it was doing, it made up a story about what it could see – namely, the chicken. It said the right hemisphere chose the shovel to clean out a chicken shed.[88]

While the entire narrative is fascinating, the last sentence is of greatest interest here. With the physical and verbal operations taking place in separate, disconnected parts of the brain, the subject was unable to explain why the chicken was chosen. So the subject's ultraconscious immediately stepped in, lying both to the researcher *and to the subject*.

A similar phenomenon has been observed when electric stimulation was applied to the motor cortex in preparation for brain surgery. As the electrode touched the place that controls arm movement, for example, the patient's arm would jerk involuntarily, but the patient would immediately say she meant to move her arm and fabricate a logical explanation. For example, she was waving to the nurse walking by the door.

The ability to make things up, including false memories that the person subsequently accepts as true, is unique to the left hemisphere of the human brain, researchers have learned. It's a trait that becomes particularly obvious in split-brain patients. "When presented with new information, people usually remember much of what they experience," the researchers wrote. "When questioned, they also usually claim to remember things that are not truly part of the experience. If split-brain patients are given such tests, the left hemisphere generates many false reports."[89]

The most important implication for our purposes: the left brains of *all* people stand ready to make things up ultraconsciously, then send these lies to the conscious – where they are believed without question.

Dissociative Identity Disorder. Also known as multiple personality, split personality and sometimes mislabeled as schizophrenia, dissociative identity disorder is defined by the American Psychiatric Association as manifesting these characteristics:

A.   The presence of two or more distinct identities or personality states (each with its own relatively enduring pattern of perceiving, relating to, and thinking about the environment and self).

B.   At least two of these identities or personality states recurrently take control of the person's behavior.

C.   Inability to recall important personal information that is too extensive to be explained by ordinary forgetfulness.

D.   The disturbance is not due to the direct physiological effects of a substance (e.g., blackouts or chaotic behavior during Alcohol Intoxication) or a general medical condition (e.g., complex partial seizures). Note: In children, the symptoms are not attributable to imaginary playmates or other fantasy play.[90]

Put simply, dissociative identity disorder (also discussed in Secret 2 as a method the ultraconscious uses to enable the conscious to cope with pain) happens when two or more people live in the same mind and, often, don't know about each other.

We might dismiss the disorder as too strange to comprehend, but I propose it is less an unexplainable oddity than another proof –

albeit an extreme one – of the human ultraconscious's ability to tell fantastic lies and have them passed off quite easily as truth.

We already know that the ultraconscious can create fantasy worlds in our dreams, and can lie to us about pain and about our motivations for doing things. Dissociative identity disorder indicates a deceptive power at another order of magnitude, conjuring two people within the same body and brain and hiding them from each other.

He may not have created two personalities in your particular brain, but the fact he can should earn him your respect, fear and vigilant attention.

Cognitive Dissonance. What happens if you believe a certain thing but end up doing something that contradicts that belief? For example, perhaps you know smoking is bad for you but are hooked on cigarettes. Or you are asked to perform a boring, repetitive task and don't get paid for it. The result is "cognitive dissonance," an uncomfortable state where your beliefs don't match your behaviors. Leon Festinger coined the phrase in the 1950s. His theories about it launched a broad new area of psychological inquiry.

Researchers discovered that disagreements between one's conscious beliefs and what one is actually doing can create anxiety, guilt and stress – but that these unpleasant feelings are often resolved by some process other than conscious logic.

In one oft-replicated study,[91] people are paid varying amounts of money to write an essay that disagrees with their beliefs. People paid more money to write the essay experience less cognitive dissonance. They wrote what they did for the money only, they'll say. But those paid a relatively small amount are less comfortable with what they're being asked to do and struggle to justify the behavior. Sometimes, those in the latter group will actually change their opinion to conform with what they write. In other words, if you do something that doesn't make sense based on your beliefs, you will (presumably with the help of your ultraconscious) adjust your opinions and beliefs to match your behavior.

The significance here is not that you're changing your mind – that happens often enough. The concept is important because it suggests people are changing their minds about important things without any conscious activity. Your ultraconscious doesn't like cognitive dissonance for his own reasons, and if alleviating them means he needs to manufacture a new belief system for you, so be it.

Preconceptions. Among its many other talents, the human mind is a rapid-fire judgment machine, evaluating everything you see and reaching conclusions with very little conscious input. Jonathan Haidt and Selin Kesebir reviewed a collection of research that demonstrates that the brain instantly evaluates everything from "irregular polygons and Chinese ideographs" to a wide array of human attributes, including trustworthiness, morality and various personality traits.

The emphasis for this human judgment mechanism, Haidt and Kesebir assert, seems to be on speed and consistency, not accuracy or an appreciation of modern morality.

> (T)he story has been consistent: People form an initial evaluation of social objects almost instantly, and these evaluations are hard to inhibit or change by conscious will-power. Even when people engage in moral reasoning, they do so in a mental space that has already been prestructured by intuitive processes, including affective reactions which prepare the brain to approach or avoid the person or proposition being considered." [92]

Or, to put the same thought in the context of this chapter: Your ultraconscious has already decided the value of everything, using rules, principles and processing you aren't aware of and cannot fully control, and he will tell you how to feel – about an idea, an event or another person. Whether he's deciding in according with your modern sense of right and wrong is irrelevant. You might want to apply your personal morality to the complicated questions of life in today's world – but he'll do what he can to make sure that doesn't happen, to, in effect, hold your attempt to be good hostage to the laws of the jungle.

Patternicity. The world is a confusing, mysterious place to your ultraconscious. As brilliant as he is, he cannot know at your birth the behavior of every insect, reptile, bird and mammal. He doesn't know what plants poison or nourish. He doesn't know the particular social rules of the group you were born into, or the opportunities or threats presented by other groups. So he must observe, note cause and effect and, where possible, bring you into the loop so you'll respond instantly when there's a danger or you're about to do something dumb.

If one family in your community boils their water, and they are the only people who don't get dysentery, you'll decide that boiling water prevents illness and you'll start doing it too. In a pre-modern society, neither you nor your ultraconscious would know anything about microorganisms and have no idea why boiling water is helpful – you just do it because you've noticed it seems to have a good effect.

In a study of the benefits of identifying correct cause-effect relationships versus the costs of seeing relationships where they don't exist, researchers Kevin Foster and Hanna Kokko concluded that it's better to find lots of relationships, even if many of them are false, than to not see any relationships, some fraction of which will be both true and relevant to survival. "(N)atural selection can favor strategies that lead to frequent errors in assessment as long as the occasional correct response carries a large fitness benefit,"[93] they wrote.

In other words, it's better to spit out good food 100 times because you think it's poisonous than to swallow poison once; better to run from a shadow you think is a tiger 100 times than to stumble into the beast once.

Observes Michael Shermer, author of *How We Believe*, "We are the descendants of those most successful at finding patterns. (O)ur brains are belief engines: evolved pattern-recognition machines that connect the dots and create meaning out of the patterns that we think we see in nature. Sometimes A really is connected to B; sometimes it is not. Unfortunately, we did not evolve a Baloney Detection Network in the brain to distinguish between true and false patterns. We have no error-detection governor to modulate the pattern-recognition engine."[94]

Conflict. How many human beings through the ages have gone to war, filed a lawsuit or fought with a neighbor, armed with nothing but the absolute certainty of the rightness of their cause?

Surely, you have been in a few conflicts yourself, and can attest to the logic-based conviction of rightness that floods your mind. If you were paying attention, you may have noticed the equally devout certitude of those on the other side.

Whenever two people disagree, at least one of them must be wrong. Therefore, at least half the people involved in every one of the countless disputes taking place on planet earth right now are wrong.

That's a lot of people. But most of them, wielding an ultraconscious that lies to them and shields them from reality for his own purposes, don't perceive the cognitive errors in the same way they don't necessarily know what's going on in their bodies.

A Hunting Trip with the Ultraconscious. There will be no quiz on the list you've just read of ultraconscious lies, distortions, obfuscations and misdirections. My intention was to impart just two data points, first, that the lies you and the rest of us are subjected to from within are sweeping and comprehensive, and second, that these lies are happening for various reasons, from helpful to counter-productive to utterly self-destructive. Some lies, such as patternicity and preconception, might be useful to you in a dark alley or the jungle, should you spend much time in either place. Some lies, such as cognitive dissonance, are less benign. While they might help us avoid conflict and conform safely to a confusing, dangerous world, they are a hindrance to improving our lives through the courageous, rational pursuit of truth – a pursuit the modern world is uniquely able to facilitate, with its ready access to information and many paths for productive, non-violent conflict resolution.

Other lies are completely out of place in the modern world, particularly strategic cognitive self-ignorance. As useful as it might have been in the forest 20,000 years ago, our ability to lie to ourselves today is a vast generator of misery.

Imagine for a moment that you are a prehistoric hunter, out pursuing game in the hopes of feeding your family for another few days. You see a deer and let your arrow fly. Did you hit it? Maybe. You follow it through the brush. Minutes later, you come upon it, dead and lying on its side. There is an arrow deep in its shoulder.

Delighted, you grab a leg and start dragging. You've barely moved the deer two feet, however, when a hostile voice barks out just behind you.

"That's my kill!"

You recognize the speaker as an acquaintance from another tribe. Perhaps you've done some trading with his people, maybe even swapped mates at some point, but right now, in this forest, your evolved brain is flooded with an overwhelming emotional cocktail of rage and self-righteousness, powered of course by the certainty that this slain deer is *your* kill.

The interloper (let's call him Albert) reaches for the arrow that brought the animal down. If you studied it for even the briefest moment, you would know it wasn't one of yours. But you don't study, you simply rip it out of the carcass before Albert can get to it and throw it into the brush.

Albert hops over the deer and retrieves the arrow, still dripping with deer blood. He shakes it in your face. "My arrow!" he cries.

However, no amount of evidence or logic can change your mind at this point, thanks to the lying intervention of your ultraconscious. You laugh ironically, pull a fresh arrow out of your quiver and give it a good shake. "My arrow!" you counter. "Get away from my dinner, you thief!"

You and Albert are about the same height and build, but Albert sees in your eyes an intimidating mix of anger, determination and absolute certainty. Had there been even a hint of self-doubt in your mind, it might have shown, and Albert would have kept arguing or perhaps even thrown a punch. It's obvious to him that *you* are the thief, but knowledge in that day was of little use against someone so unwavering in his cause, no matter how dubious.

Albert backs away with a curse, you get the deer and your family eats for another week. Your children have inherited from you the same ability for self-deception, and when they argue with Albert's offspring in the woods, they will win, just as you did. They will win and breed, and Albert's descendents will die hungry and childless.

Now, let's bring this argument into the modern day. It's you and Albert again, but now you're modern people, arguing about a loan, a piece of land, damage to a car, something at work, a political dispute. Because the ability for strategic cognitive self-deception has been selected by evolution for all human minds, both of you are now blessed with the ability of absolute faith in your position.

In this case, as in that argument long ago in the woods, you are wrong and Albert is right. There's not a bloody arrow, but there are papers you have signed, or witnesses who saw things, or incriminating paint smears on your bumper. You can't see these things, unfortunately, or add them to a comprehensive understanding of your case vs. the case of Albert, because your ultraconscious won't let you. This is how you used to win arguments, after all, and your ultraconscious doesn't know things have changed. Or, more accurately, his evolution hasn't caught up with the modern world. The process of evolution is slow while the march of human progress has been remarkably speedy of late, and humans with instincts for a more modern, fact-based sense of true and false, right and wrong, have not yet evolved.

So off you go, figuratively shaking your arrow in Albert's face, certain of your case as he presents his own bloody arrow to the authorities.

There were no authorities in the jungle, but now they are everywhere. Police, judges, juries, commissioners, supervisors, prosecutors, arbitrators, journalists. Even modern sports are under the strict control of this essential class of people – referees, line judges, umpires. These authorities, furthermore, possess unprecedented fact-gathering powers. They dust for fingerprints, scan photographs and video footage, analyze chemicals, interview witnesses, pore over contracts with the help of word-search software. Your absolute certainty is of zero consequence to them. If the facts don't support your case, you lose. And lose big, sometimes, getting stuck with huge fines, imprisonment, court costs and attorney's fees and, should you be involved in a high-profile dispute, public humiliation.

Had you taken a hard look at your claims vs. Albert's – had you been able to override the certainty your ultraconscious had imposed on you – you might have settled out of court, thrown yourself on your foe's mercy, apologized and gone on with your life. Instead, you walked arm in arm with your ultraconscious into disaster, a catastrophe engineered long ago in a world that no longer exists.

Now, imagine that you are not simply a private citizen with an argument over a dead deer or some other triviality, but the leader of a large, well-armed nation. As powerful as you might be, you are still burdened with the same anachronistic ultraconscious as the rest of us, so when you and Albert disagree and you are convinced of your unquestionable rightness, there will be war. And there is nothing quite like war to deprive people of happiness.

Emotional Lies

We have talked so far about your ultraconscious' ability to fool your physical senses and confuse your abilities to gather and process truth, but there's more. Yes, he can lie about what you're sensing physically and distort your ability to think through the fact and logic of your existence, but these are minor tools next to his most powerful weapon – your emotions.

So important are your emotions to everything you do, it's fair to wonder why your ultraconscious even bothers controlling your pain and your logical processing. The simple, chilling answer is most likely that evolution always favored complete conformance to the requirements of reproduction, not just partial conformance or extensive conformance. Today, the human conscious arrives as the inheritor of an ancient, perfectly–engineered totalitarianism, living its life under the complete authority of a despot far more powerful than any of history's most successful autocrats.

George Orwell's *1984* introduced the term "thoughtcrime," a misdeed taking place only in the mind that challenges the order of things and is therefore a punishable offense.

But truly, the oppressed subjects of Orwell's dystopian society had it easy, for at least they had the freedom to commit thoughtcrime. Those of us living under the thumb of an ultraconscious rarely get that far. We don't perceive the oppression, because it comes from within. Or if we do perceive it, we don't understand it because until this generation the science wasn't there. And then, science and perception aside, there is emotion, and that is your ultraconscious' trump card.

"Psychoanalysis has taught us that our intellect is a feeble thing, a tool of our instincts," Freud wrote in 1905, "and that we are all compelled to behave cleverly or stupidly by the commands of our emotional attitudes."

A year or two before he took his life in 1890, the painter Vincent Van Gogh wrote, "small emotions are the great captains of our lives."

Agreed Baruch Spinoza, the 17th century Dutch philosopher, "when a man is a prey to his emotions, he is not his own master, but lies at the mercy of fortune: so much so, that he is often compelled, while seeing that which is better for him, to follow that which is worse."[95]

You are allowed a little thought, a little logic. You couldn't read this book without it. But the moment your ultraconscious decides he needs to take charge, he'll assign an emotion, typically in the form of a chemical, that shuts off everything else. Dopamine, serotonin, epinephrine, norepinephrine, γ-aminobutyric acid and countless more emotion-directing chemicals swirl together among your neurons in a complex interplay of physical and mental directives.

Rage, ecstasy, jealousy, lust, hurt, infatuation – these are the extremes of your emotional existence. And unless you're willing and able to resist them, *they are completely out of your control.* Do you decide when to feel anger, or is it up to what others do and how your ultraconscious orders you to respond? Do you schedule your jealousy for certain convenient times of the day? Do you feel infatuation only after you have carefully considered all the most important attributes of the person of interest? Or is it instantaneous, coming from someplace outside your conscious, as involuntary as breathing or blinking your eyes? Cupid wields a bow and arrow, after all, not a checklist.

Consider pre-menstrual syndrome, the monthly ordeal of fertile women. Emotional symptoms – set by the calendar, not by anything actually going on in life – include hostility, depression, anger, mistrust and anxiety. While it is one of the more regular afflictions of humankind, it is certainly not the only instance where emotions are assigned independent of what's actually happening. Indeed, when you awake and wonder what the world will give and take away on this new day, you should also wonder what emotions the ultraconscious is going to assign.

"(F)eelings," writes Pascal Boyer, "are the outcome of complex calculations that specialized systems in our minds carry out in precise terms."[96]

I have been writing about strong emotions, but what about the lesser ones? Why do you like certain people and dislike others? How much does it have to do with the good and bad they do to you, versus something less measurable? Chances are, you have a preference for certain kinds of music, paintings, homes, jokes, jobs, neighborhoods, books, movies, cities, cars, restaurants, gods and news, and dislike many other varieties of these things that other people prefer. And chances are, you have never stopped to understand why you prefer what you do.

And yet, the unexamined, unexplainable emotions are telling you what to do continuously, throughout your day, throughout your life. You are the fiddle and your ultraconscious, manipulating you through your emotions, is playing his own music with you. You may think you are pursuing happiness, but you are wrong. You are simply the vehicle your ultraconscious drives as he journeys toward his final destination, the only destination that – thanks to the rules of evolution – matters to him: maximum offspring. He decides what you sense, how you think and how you feel about things. He does not care about your happiness, except as another of the many tools he uses to make you do what he wants.

Your capacity for self-delusion puts you at risk across the spectrum of life, from the trivial decisions you make day-to-day to the great themes of your life. In *The Hidden Brain*, Shankar Vedantam describes the process by which the systematic inculcation of delusion creates people willing to murder, commit atrocities and die for any cause. He writes of the Kamikaze pilots who flew their planes into ships during WWII, suicide bombers around the world who do their work in the name of both religious and secular goals, and the mass suicide in Jonestown, Guyana, in 1978, where almost 1,000 people killed themselves under orders of Jim Jones, their megalomaniacal leader.

In each case, Vedantam compares the indoctrination process to a tunnel where the brain's ability to ignore important information and believe nonsense is exploited by leaders who are power-mad, on the take or suffering under their own delusions.

"When we think of suicide bombers as crazed and evil fanatics, we are applying our norms to their behavior," Vedantam writes. "But inside the tunnel, the world has been turned upside down. Our norms no longer apply."[97]

Vedantam compares these deluded ones to those who commit a slower form of suicide, working a hundred hours a week for the good of the corporation, or in the belief the distant payoff will somehow be worth the neglected children, divorce and years of meaningless toil.

I met such a person soon after I graduated from college, when I applied for a job as a salesman at Radio Shack and was interviewed by Bob, the district manager. Bob spent a great deal of time talking about himself during the interview, perhaps for the same reason that other types of fanatics focus on themselves: to reinforce their beliefs and drown out conflicting thoughts. I learned that Bob was working from 7 a.m. to 10 p.m. six days a week, and that Radio Shack produced more millionaires than any other American corporation. He hoped to become one of them, he said. And his ultimate goal, he declared, was a big Greco-Roman house.

Married and a father, with a family he rarely saw, he had deluded himself into the endless pursuit of a building he would rarely occupy.

Your experiences, the things you think, believe and feel, are often irrelevant illusions. Irrelevant to reality. Irrelevant to your happiness.

All of us have been grievously fooled.

"Feed Them Shit"

The idea that your feelings, thoughts and emotions are, to a large degree, irrelevant to your conscious existence and pursuit of happiness may, quite naturally, be impossible for you to believe. How could you or any organism operate this way, its systems for directing its activities split into multiple sections that often work against each other?

"A house divided against itself cannot stand," insisted Jesus.

But there is a parallel for such a model of direction, in the form of large organizations. Governments and corporations, even the successful ones, are often found making official claims that they do things one way while their actual behaviors are quite different. Time and again, a president, CEO or member of a corporate board confesses to ignorance of some questionable practice or behavior lower down in the organization that is common, long-term and often quite beneficial to the organization. Often enough, their expressions of ignorance appear to be honest. They may truly believe that everyone in the company is working toward the corporate mission statement of serving customers with the highest integrity, at the same time that the employees are maintaining success and profitability by skirting laws, misleading customers and ignoring corporate policies.

A 2006 scandal at computer maker Hewlett-Packard comes to mind. Seeking to identify the source of leaks of sensitive corporate information, top officers at the firm hired security experts to help find out who was spilling the beans. These experts then hired private investigators who broke the law, using illegal software and impersonating journalists and members of the Hewlett-Packard board to find the leaker. When the scandal broke, top executives at the firm expressed shock, surprise and a general ignorance of what was being done. A September, 2006 article in USA Today portrayed a corporate house divided, noting that of 14 key figures in the spying scandal summoned to testify before Congress, "not one claimed responsibility . . . Former chairman Patricia Dunn, who was involved with the program early and ran it at a high level . . . insisted that she was culpable only of trusting well-respected subordinates. 'I do not accept personal responsibility for what happened,' she said."[98]

Also testifying, CEO Mark Hurd acknowledged error and wrongdoing but, like Dunn, implied he just didn't know what was going on. "I should have been able to catch (the problem)," he said. "I didn't."

Both may have been lying, but it's just as likely they approved of the spying program but remained ignorant of its details, in the same way you might remain ignorant of how your ultraconscious pursues your reproductive self-interest.

A saying has arisen about how to treat other individuals and groups at a large organization: "Treat them like mushrooms," it goes. "Keep them in the dark and feed them shit." When I looked up the expression on the internet, I found it being used everywhere, boards of directors giving rank and file employees the mushroom treatment, employees and mid-level managers feeding shit to the top brass, CEOs keeping boards of directors and employees in the dark.

Your ultraconscious, apparently, is doing the same thing, lying to you – the CEO of your life and body – about what's really happening while he feeds you a stream of false memories, erroneous logic and involuntary emotions that have nothing to do with what's going on around you but enable him to do what works best from his perspective.

How Understanding Secret 3 Might Make You Happier

There's at least a book's worth of advice one could glean from the notion that your brain is lying to you across the spectrum of cognitive and emotional experiences.

But I'll limit my advice here to two critical topics: selling to other people and fighting with other people more effectively. Together, these two areas of life make up a huge share of what you do with your life, and effectiveness at both will help you in critical ways to get what you want. Mates and friends, the cooperation of those around you, financial security, these are the central ingredients of happiness, and getting them requires the ability to sell, and to prevail when fighting is necessary.

When selling, you must know your customer. You must ask questions, understand what they want and then figure out if you have anything to offer them.

There are opportunities to sell everywhere, not only for an organization that needs revenue, but also within your family, in your neighborhood, when you're trying to get a job or a bargain or enlist someone's help in any sort of endeavor.

The ultraconscious, unfortunately, is a poor salesman.

He prefers simply to win, and to fool you into thinking you're right when you're not. He'll form judgments about the people you're trying to appeal to without any actual facts, he'll make you think that talking past them or over them is all you need, and when they disagree with what you're proposing, he'll order up an emotion – anger, defensiveness, anxiety, paranoia – states which make persuasion difficult or impossible.

Overriding your ultraconscious' inherent sales incompetence means starting not with lectures or arguments but with questions, and with acceptance at the outset that you might lose – that the person you're selling to or trying to persuade might never come around to your side, and might have valid reasons for staying put. Your ultraconscious won't like it, either the reliance on questions instead of brute force, or the possibility of defeat instead of victory at all costs, but there are many demands he places on you that you can train yourself to resist. It just takes practice.

Now, what about fighting?

Some of the same principles apply: Understand your opponent, ask them questions to that end (if they'll speak to you), and prepare to lose.

If you are in a serious dispute, with a co-worker, family member, neighbor or someone you're suing, force yourself to accept, just for a moment, that you are wrong. You should notice, at the moment of acceptance, a deep discomfort, instant anxiety, an emotional lurch, and possibly even physical unpleasantness – a sudden sourness in your chest, perhaps, or something like butterflies in your stomach. These are the prods of your ultraconscious, insisting from inside your mind not to think this way. "Don't go there," he's begging you. "We'll die if you do."

He'll warn you of all the horrors of giving up. You will be ostracized from the tribe. Others will perceive you as misguided and unable to prevail and will no longer present you with the best cuts of meat and the most fertile mates. Albert will get the deer and you and your children will die of starvation somewhere in the wilderness.

Or, more likely, none of this will happen. It's all just the illusion of an ultraconscious who doesn't know of the modern world or your place in it. Yes, you might lose a friend or two. You might have to pay a fine. You might even have to change jobs. But you will not starve or be exiled to the wilderness, and if you continue to fight a misguided war, the alternative may be worse.

Are you fighting frequently? Are you losing some of these fights, or most of them? Or are you winning, but at the cost of alienating family, friends, lovers, business associates? And is there a chance your ultraconscious is part of the problem, forcing you into battles because he thinks life is still a desperate contest in an unregulated jungle?

Ironically, switching to a fact-based conflict approach will win more fights for you, even if you have to concede defeat in your present conflicts. Focusing on ferreting out the truths your ultraconscious has hidden from you will help you concentrate on those battles you are most likely to win, preventing distraction and the waste of resources. You will fight less often and, inevitably, more effectively and more victoriously.

The most important moments in life often come when we realize we have been lied to – by a spouse, an employer, a religious figure. These moments are often very painful and can frequently be followed by further unpleasantness – divorce, job loss, the abandonment of certain hopes and dreams. But few people who have been disillusioned would choose to go back to their deceived state. Fortunately the removal of the wool is often followed by something better – a new or better-behaved spouse, a new job, more realistic expectations of life.

In the same way, there is both pain and opportunity in learning that that the greatest and most frequent lies you've been told have been emanating from right behind your own eyes.

You can question what you believe, challenge your emotions and take another shot at understanding the perspectives of those you hate. The outcomes might very well be quite beneficial – less conflict, more peace, better decisions and, obviously, more happiness.

There's nothing easy about this, of course. You have been designed not to know what's going on in your body. You can't think for yourself. You are pummeled by chemically-induced emotions at every turn. And unfortunately, your ultraconscious isn't finished with you yet. He's got another trick up his sleeve.

Secret 4: Your Ultraconscious Doesn't Believe in God (But He Wants You To)

According to Wikipedia, earth holds as many as 2.1 billion Christians, 1.5 billion Muslims, 1.5 billion Buddhists and 1 billion Hindus.[99] Millions more belong to other faiths, including Judaism, Sikhism, folk religions, paganism, animism and on and on. The number of distinct religions observed today is difficult to estimate, but I've seen guesses of as many as 4,200 different supernatural belief systems.

Many of the adherents of these faiths are certain of the absolute truth of their way and of the falseness of all other faiths. To date, however, none of these religions have been proven by science. No religion has been able to predict the future, win all wars, cure any disease or confer exceptional power or goodness upon its followers. Most of them claim to do all these things, but all of them seem to succeed – at war, illness, power or goodness – at about the same rate as mathematical probabilities suggest they should.

All religions are minorities – tiny minorities, in fact, if you narrow down each religion to all its various sects, e.g. Catholic Christianity, Shia Islam or Zen Buddhism. So even if one religion, or one sect of that religion, is true, the vast majority of humanity – all but the minority of that one true faith's adherents – believes lies.

The predominance of religion does not prove god. Religion proves instead that the human brain possesses a near-universal inclination toward superstition.

Why? Why is religion, in its countless, mutually-exclusive forms, so common? Why, furthermore, is it so powerful? Given the inescapable logic that no more than one religion can be true, why have so many people – around the world and throughout history – killed, suffered and died for faiths that are untrue?

And, most importantly to this book, how does the average human being's bizarre affection for the supernatural affect happiness?

Let's take a quick look at the why first, and then consider the more important how.

Why Is There Religion, and it is Useful?

Theories abound on the question of why humans believe in gods, and no definitive answer has yet emerged. In *Religion Explained*, Pascal Boyer proposes that the brain comes equipped with a variety of evolved structures that incline us to have faith in things we can't prove scientifically. We prefer to ascribe important events to an agent, for example, and if a human can't be found, our minds are quite comfortable blaming something non-human – a god, spirit, witch, deceased ancestor etc.[100]

"When people have thoughts about gods or spirits or ancestors," Boyer writes, "a whole machinery of complex mental devices is engaged, most of which is completely outside conscious access."[101]

Religion, Boyer and many others assert, is an inevitable by-product of the human mind's evolutionary design. It's an accident, in other words.

But is religion more than an accident? Is it merely a random set of behaviors resulting from the brain's particular makeup, or might it be something that, at one time long ago perhaps, helped us survive and reproduce?

If we were able to test this theory by going back in time to the dawn of religious awakening among our forebears, we would look for instances where religious beliefs and behaviors – no matter how outlandish or obviously false – enabled them to survive and reproduce while their non-religious counterparts perished childless.

We can't go back in time, but we can speculate, imagine and consult a large and growing body of research and data.

Hope. In a regrettable but inescapably useful experiment, mice were put in water and left to drown, some in utter darkness, some with a sliver of light overhead. On average, the mice who had a little light swam longer than the mice in darkness. Light overhead gave the mice something to live for, apparently, at least a little longer.

Now, let's imagine a colony of 100 mice living in a dry lake bed. The rains come one dark night and fill the mice's range with three feet of water. All 100 mice are now swimming frantically, but 10 of the mice are blessed with a psychological mutation that makes them see light where there is none. These deluded mice keep swimming while their non-mutated comrades give up, one by one, and sink hopelessly beneath the waves.

Just in the nick of time, the lakebed drains and the mice who saw the non-existent light are saved. They might be deluded – they might see light in the darkness – but they are alive, and in the cold calculus of earthly existence, that's all that matters.

Now let's replace the mice with ancient humans, and the flood with any of the calamities that might befall us in our formative eons: a vicious enemy, famine, disease, infertility, fire or, of course, flood. And let's replace the non-existent light with a non-existent god. Animal spirits, tree sprites, a thunder lord, a guardian angel, Shiva, Wyrd, Odin, Zeus, Jehovah, Jesus, Allah.

Hope in these deities and in their promises kept us swimming, literally or figuratively. It increased self-confidence, which can improve performance and help in conflicts with others, as suggested in the previous secret (see Wrangham). Hope chases away depression, which can lead to suicide, compromised immune systems and reduced interest in procreation. "Be strong and take heart, all you who hope in the Lord," assures Psalm 31:34.

It was not God but the illusion of God, perhaps, that inspired our forebears to keep swimming and breeding long enough to spawn us. We are indeed indebted, not to real divinity, but to our ability to see divinity where it is not.

Reproduction. A joke: Why don't Southern Baptists approve of sex standing up? Punchline: Because it might lead to dancing.

I first heard this one when I was attending a small, Christian college in upstate South Carolina, in the heart of the American Bible Belt. The girl who told me the joke thought it was merely funny, but having grown up in more cosmopolitan Fort Lauderdale, I was mystified.

"No, really, why don't Southern Baptists approve of sex standing up?" I asked. I didn't want a punchline, I wanted an answer.

"I don't know," she replied.

"Is it a religious thing?" I persisted. "Is there something in the Bible about it?"

As humans too often do when confronted with a mystery of religious behavior, she shrugged and changed the subject. But the question lingered for me. Why would any theology concern itself with sex positions?

I'm not sure Southern Baptist theology actually forbids sex standing up (although they do have a history of opposing dancing). But there is a loud ring of truth to the joke. In fact, religion and religion-inspired laws have long concerned themselves with all things sexual. And if we look at religious rules from the perspective of their ability to maximize offspring, many odd little pieces of God's arcane will start falling into place.

The missionary position? This position (couple face to face, male on top) was favored by the medieval Catholic Church and other religious adherents because it contrasted with the baser sex positions practiced by animals, or reinforced the theme of male dominance. But it is also believed to be one of the best positions for conception (while standing is one of the worst).

Most religions prohibit homosexuality and adultery. From a reproductive perspective, the first doesn't get the job done while the second does, but at the price of an uncertain parentage, which can cause the father to withdraw from the family and take his essential time and resources with him. Incest and masturbation are forbidden or at least frowned upon by many faiths for similar reasons. The first produces unhealthy offspring, the second produces nothing at all – at least, nothing of value if the first objective of existence is reproduction.

The god of Judeo-Christian imaginings hates to death behaviors that do not lead to effective reproduction and, as we might expect, is highly supportive of those that do. He mandates death for homosexuals and adulterers and urges his people to "go forth and multiply," (Genesis 9:7). God changes Abram's name to Abraham, which means "father of many nations," (Genesis 17:5) and promises to "make your descendants as the dust of the earth; so that if a man could number the dust of the earth, then your descendants also could be numbered" (Genesis 13:16).

The concept occurs in many faiths, from prehistoric fertility cults to modern Mormonism. "It is God's plan for us to multiply and replenish the earth by having children," declares www.mormonbeliefs.org, voicing a central tenet of the faith that, statistics indicate, is dutifully followed. According to the U.S. Census Bureau, the average household size in Utah, the state with the highest percentage of Mormons per capita, was 3.19 in 2007 – the largest household headcount in the nation.

A similar philosophy is practiced by the Quiverful movement, a worldwide body of evangelist Christians who point to Psalm 127 and other Biblical verses as evidence God wants them to have a lot of babies. The website www.quiverful.com (accessed February 2011), declares itself to be "Dedicated to providing encouragement and practical help to those who are striving to raise a large and growing, godly family in today's world!"

Many faiths prohibit birth control. "Contraception is to be judged objectively so illicit," Pope John Paul II told a group of Indonesian bishops in 1980, "that it can never, for any reason be justified." (www.catholicsagainstcontraception.com).

If your brain is inclined to adopt religious beliefs that prohibit non-procreative sexuality and that insist godliness is all about making babies, you will have more children, and they will inherit brains that work like yours does.

Selfishness and Murder. The Old Testament, a core of the belief systems of billions of people around the world (Christians, Jews and Muslims all revere the book to some degree), provides an explicit chronicle of many evolutionarily beneficial behaviors, including the land grabs, genocide and mass rape performed by the Israelis under the direction of their God.

Sometimes the Israeli army killed everyone, "both man and woman, young and old," as in Jericho (Joshua 6:21), and sometimes they killed adults and boys but kept the virgins for themselves, as Moses instructed in Numbers 31:14-18.

The Abrahamic faiths are not the only ones that inspired self-beneficial theft, rape and murder, of course. Religious-based atrocity is so common around the world and through the ages it's become cliché. People kill people and take their stuff, and then they say God told them to. And they live on, have more children and give them their genes.

A Parable About a Train and a Child. Imagine you're driving with your three-year-old daughter when you wreck the car. You're pinned under the steering wheel, but to your horror, your child is able to free herself and she crawls down from her seat and out the door. Your fear grows when you notice railroad tracks nearby and hear the horn of a distant train. She is fascinated by trains: She loves watching trains go by from the safety of your lap, and visiting miniature train exhibits.

Immediately, she heads for the tracks, in complete ignorance of the danger there. You, with your decades of experience, have a complete understanding of all the terrible things that might be about to happen. You understand that trains are massive and can take more than a mile to stop. You have read countless stories about train disasters and have seen train crashes, a few real ones caught on film and many more simulated wrecks in movies and on TV.

Your daughter, at three years old, has no such knowledge. The concepts of mass, weight and stopping distance are completely foreign to her. She has never seen a train wreck, real or simulated, or read a story about what happens to someone who's been run over by a train. And as the train's horn blows again, now much closer, you know you don't have time to explain everything. And even if you had time, her brain simply isn't set up to understand. It will take years of experience and mental development before she fully understands the threat that is bearing down on her at 45 miles per hour.

The following conversation ensues:

"Honey, come back to the car."

"No, I want to see the train." (Your daughter is a little strong willed.)

"The train will hurt you."

"No it won't. I'm going to make it stop so it will help you."

"Get off the tracks!"

"No. If I do, they won't see me."

"Get off the tracks!" you shout again, but the horn blows and the train's so close now it drowns out your voice.

You realize it's time to lie, and you need to lie fast and big before the horn blares again.

"Honey, remember the winged monkeys from that movie?" you ask, thinking of something your daughter finds very frightening.

"Yes," she replies nervously.

"I think they're on that train." You look up, pretending you can see the engine. "Yes, that train has winged monkeys on it. You better come back to the car."

Without a moment's hesitation, she runs back to you. (You cover her eyes as the engine passes, of course, so she won't see the genial fellow waving from the cab)

Yes, you lied, and you are a lying liar, but your lie saved your child's life.

What does the story mean? Your daughter is your conscious, which lacks a memory or calculative abilities adequate to fully appreciating the dangers of your world. You, the parent, are your ultraconscious, much more knowledgeable of threats than your daughter but unable to communicate with her honestly and rationally. And the winged monkeys are the religion you have just created to save your daughter's life.

As your daughter grows older, she will face many more threats: men who might get her pregnant before she's ready to be a mother; substances that feel good but can kill; theft and deception that can be useful but also lead to interpersonal and legal problems. At each step along the way, you can attempt to point her in the right direction by imparting your extensive and perhaps incomprehensible (or boring) knowledge, or you can just make up more religion.

If you are her ultraconscious, you can never impart your knowledge. The vast store of memories and the billions or more operations you are performing every second will mean nothing to her. So religion it must be.

We might theorize that those whose brains mutated to foster a partnership between conscious and ultraconscious, a partnership in which he was able to make up religious principles for his own purposes and they were able to believe them without question – did so well in the ancient struggle to survive and reproduce that they prevailed, and became parents to us all.

"Having concepts of gods and spirits does not really make moral rules more *compelling* but it sometimes makes them more *intelligible*," writes Pascal Boyer in *Religion Explained*. "So we do not have gods because that makes society function. We have gods in part because we have the mental equipment that makes society possible but we cannot always understand how society functions."[102]

In summary, of the thousands of religions observed around the world, many include rules and concepts with direct implications for survival and reproduction. If you follow any particular religion, I encourage you to review its theology for elements that might have more to do with survival and reproduction than with the will of an invisible spirit.

But let's move on – how does happiness do in the hands of religion?

Does Religion Promote Happiness?

So religion creates hope. It keeps you on the straight and narrow for effective reproduction. It justifies beneficial selfishness. And it gets you to do useful but non-obvious things.

All good (at least for you and your genes, though not necessarily good for your victims or the overpopulated world). But overall, does religion serve happiness, despite the harm it can occasionally do? Is religion more like water and fire, which can drown and burn but overall are essential? Or is it more like alcohol, which creates pleasant, non-essential sensations but can ruin lives and cause death and destruction?

I'd go with alcohol.

Religion, like alcohol, does the least harm when used in moderation. The problem with religion, unlike alcohol, is that it invariably comes with a user's manual that recommends zealous over-consumption.

Fortunately, religion tends to temper itself a bit in the modern world. Most civilized people sip their faith, reconciling superstitious absolutism with their preference for comfortable, peaceful lives. Modern religion might be compared to fine wine, distilled from the rotgut that used to kill people wholesale.

So is modern religion, which has been stripped of its more unsavory characteristics, now primarily a force for happiness? If it were that simple, I wouldn't bother including this secret among the others in this book. Regrettably, the answer depends on who you are. If you don't have much trouble conforming to the rules of your particular faith, are able to enrich your social life through interactions with fellow believers, and find hope and happiness through superstition when times are tough, religion might be a good thing for you.

However, if you are a homosexual in a faith that condemns homosexuality, you may end up hating yourself and other homosexuals, and hate directed anywhere is typically not a route to happiness. If your faith permits social and romantic communion only with fellow believers, you may be missing out on valuable relationships. If your faith requires that you convert non-believers, your desire to proselytize will corrupt (and often end) worthwhile friendships. If your god always needs money (most deities have trouble handling cash, as the late comedian George Carlin pointed out), you may end up losing your financial lifeblood to, at best, meaningless lies and, at worst, hateful nonsense (e.g. the Mormon couple who gave their children's college education fund to the campaign for banning gay marriage in California).

If you are devoting yourself to the study of theology, not just for amusement or as a mental exercise but because you believe it represents absolute truth, you are missing out on things that are much more likely to be true. If your faith gives you the hope that God will solve your problems without your active participation, you are headed for the misery of failure. If you believe, like countless people of many faiths for millennia have, that the world will end in your lifetime and your god is coming back in a blaze of glory, you are probably going to neglect the work that must be done for the sake of a troubled world that isn't going to mend itself. And every day he doesn't come will be slightly more disappointing.

If you believe that your fellow faith travelers are more virtuous, more blessed, or in some way uniquely empowered or guided by a god or some other spiritual force, you are in danger of exploitation at their hands.

If you cannot regard the universe and the people in it without a religious overlay, you are depriving yourself of enjoying the universe in its naked, unvarnished and profoundly wondrous form.

How Understanding Secret 4 Might Make You Happier

The ability of this chapter to change your life is directly proportional to how superstitious you are. If you are an atheist, you probably could have skipped this secret altogether. If you are a zealot who tries to conform your entire existence to the will of one

or more mythic beings, recognizing your beliefs for what they are –
and abandoning them – will be deeply transformative.

I have no illusions. If you are a zealot who is very
comfortable in the absolute truths you believe you have found, you
probably wouldn't have picked up this book to start with, or would
have set it down quickly once you realized what it was about.

The ultraconscious does not like to be disturbed.

If you do however harbor some religious faith but not so
much that books like this are verboten, ask yourself some questions,
and write down your answers (the ultraconscious hates it when you
put things in writing).

Have you eschewed friendship or a romantic relationship
because of your religious beliefs? How much time and money have
you given to your faith, and has the return on that investment, in the
form of happiness, been comparable to other things you have (or
could have) invested in? Are you in charge of your own life, or are
you doing the bidding of your deity, or your deity's self-appointed
representatives on earth? Are you trying to fix your life, or the
world, or waiting for a supreme being to come and make things
better?

An extraterrestrial who'd reached this point in this book
would likely be amazed at how difficult it is to be a human. And
we're not finished yet.

Secret 5: Stupidity: It's a Feature, Not a Bug!

In the 1999 movie *The Sixth Sense,* a troubled boy tells his therapist, "I see dead people."

Soon after the movie's release, t-shirts appeared proclaiming, "I see dumb people."

A spoof of *Star Trek* with a similar theme has appeared on bumper stickers and elsewhere: "Beam me up, Scotty, there's no intelligent life down here."

As brilliant as humans might be, there is an enduring sense among homo sapiens that many other members of our species are profoundly stupid. Consider the number of words invented in English to help us precisely label our dimmest fellows:

> imbecile, moron, idiot, ignoramus, fool, dummy, dumbbell (and variations dumbass and dumbfuck), dolt, dodo, oaf, lunkhead, luddite, shithead, dimwit, nitwit, halfwit, numbskull, knucklehead, pinhead, bonehead, lamebrain, pea brain, dunce, blockhead, etc.

According to legend, the Inuit peoples of Alaska have dozens of words for snow because they are surrounded by so much of it. The myth has been debunked but is still instructive: the more of something we have in our lives, the more names we must make up for it, in all its forms and nuances. Based on word count, at least, the esteemed human race is frightfully unintelligent.

Are we really that dumb? We've invented computers, rockets, medicine and laser-guided missiles, after all. Of course, all that took anatomically and mentally modern humans more than 100,000 years.

Your brain comprises 200 billion brain cells connected trillions of ways, and can conduct trillions or quadrillions of operations per second as it performs complex math and remembers things in incredible detail from years ago. So why can't you remember people's names, the things you learn at school or even the few items you were supposed to pick up at the store?

Time and again, even the geniuses of the human race make grievous mistakes of logic and calculation. "How could I have been so stupid?" is a constant refrain in the human experience.

Consider:

NASA lost a $125 million Mars orbiter because one team used English units of measurement while another team used the more conventional metric system for a key spacecraft operation, according to a review finding . . . After a 286-day journey . . . the spacecraft came within 60 km (36 miles) of the planet – about 100 km closer than planned. (T)he spacecraft's propulsion system overheated and was disabled . . . so (the craft) likely plowed through the atmosphere, continued out beyond Mars and now could be orbiting the sun . . .[103]

The Wikipedia article about Albert Einstein, when I checked it in November 2009, listed 16 of his most significant errors, including this one committed in 1922: "Einstein published a qualitative theory of superconductivity based on the vague idea of electrons shared in orbits. This paper predated modern quantum mechanics, and is well understood to be completely wrong."

Thomas Edison, who patented the phonograph, the light bulb and motion pictures (among many other brilliant inventions) fought for years to keep direct current as the standard method of electricity distribution, despite its clear inferiority to alternating current (He may have had business reasons for doing so, but really, does that matter?).

And then of course, there's war. Whenever two people disagree, at least one of them must be wrong. War is in its essence the wholesale, intentional killing of human beings by other human beings due to someone's error.

How can we, with our mighty minds, possibly be such screw ups? How could evolution have permitted us brains with such a propensity for destructive, wasteful and fatal mistakes?

If we look at the human brain as the world's ultimate software, we must conclude it's got a serious bug: stupidity.

All software has bugs, those maddening little quirks that make it difficult or impossible to get something important done. In several versions of Microsoft Excel I used in the 1990's, for example, I needed to sum a column of if-then statements. If a number in an adjacent cell was under a certain value, I programmed the cell in my if-then column to return a 0. If the number were higher than that value, the if-then cell would give a 1. So how many 0's did I have, and how many 1's? I never found out. Excel did not recognize the number 1 in an if-then formula as an actual 1, and refused to add them. The sum of my if-then column was always 0.

Software marketers have a ready answer for the bugs people find in their software. "It's not a bug," they'll say. "It's a feature!"

It's not a flaw in the software, in other words. It's something we put in there on purpose, to be helpful. It it's not helping you, it's probably your fault. By the same token, if your stupidity isn't helping you, you're just not understanding the value of stupidity.

Imagine a soul who is ready to occupy a physical form and is picking out body parts in a department store. After she chooses her face, her torso, her legs and hands, she floats over to the brain department, viewing the brains of hundreds of sentient species who have evolved around the universe. Finally, she arrives at the earth brain, net weight three pounds, a gray, wrinkled, two-lobed, symmetrical lump being peddled by a slick software salesman.

"Now this little beauty is a real problem solver," he tells her. "It's got hundreds of modules, or maybe thousands. More than we can count, I'll tell you that. Billions of brain cells! Quadrillions of operations every second! It hates, it loves, it does quantum mechanics, sometimes all in the same day!"

"I've heard about earth brains," the soul says. "They're not very bright, are they?"

"Intelligence is overrated," the salesman counters. "Best kept secret in the universe. Stupidity is not a bug, it's a feature! You want to survive and breed? Dumbness! That's your ticket."

Could he be right? Is the human brain's stupidity bug actually a feature, something that evolved because it was useful?

Conscious Stupidity: A Theory

As has been noted earlier in this book, your brain evolved to give you maximum intelligence in the world where your brain evolved. And that world was very, very different from the world you inhabit now. The modern world is so new, humans have not yet evolved to live effectively in it. None of us are born with the natural intelligence required for modern life.

It's a profound point: We are not yet intelligent enough to live in the world created by our intelligence.

It takes us decades of painstaking study for each of us to learn the facts required to understand and maintain even a small part of modern society's operations. We can't remember simple lists of items, or the vital steps of an important process, meaning tragically common, sometimes fatal errors in fields as diverse as surgery, building maintenance, aeronautics and statecraft.

I propose here that it may not be just a failure to evolve that condemns us to dumbness. Dumbness, I theorize, represents the *culmination* of human intellectual evolution.

Ancient humans, as has been noted previously, lacked much of the knowledge that you take for granted. They could not read, there was no science, and they had access only to those rare shreds of information that others offered or they uncovered on their own. Every human of old, however, was issued an extremely powerful ultraconscious, able to store vast amounts of information, calculate probabilities and, quite likely, do other math we can barely imagine.

So the most successful ancient humans were not the people best at consciously figuring out solutions to problems. Success, in the form of survival and reproduction, went to the ones best at obeying the dictates of the ultraconscious without question. If the ultraconscious, with his amazing data and calculative abilities, told them something, he was probably right. When the ultraconscious commanded a certain emotion – lust, envy, jealousy or murderous rage – it was best to simply believe without question. Those who accepted his lies, about our bodies, our minds, other people, gods, went on to inherit the earth.

Success in the ancient world didn't require logic, concentration, conscious problem-solving or technological experience. Instead, it demanded an instant, unquestioning faith in the hunches, intuition, passions and superstitions that the ultraconscious sent the conscious. We are stupid because evolution favored those *too stupid to challenge or compete with their own ultraconsciouses.*

There is considerable evidence that our stupidity is not a natural result of something about the way the brain cells of the conscious must operate, but is instead artificial, imposed by a variety of internal and external forces. Consider:

Verbal Overshadowing. In one experiment, when research subjects were asked to do something the brain typically takes care of outside the conscious realm, such as solving a difficult problem through insight, the subjects did significantly worse when they were asked to talk about the thought process.

"(S)ubjects who attempted to verbalize how they had been trying to solve insight problems solved significantly fewer problems than control subjects who engaged in an unrelated activity for an equivalent period of time,"[104] read a summary of one study lead by Jonathan Schooler.

The recall of faces is a profoundly difficult task that even the most advanced of today's computers struggle to perform with anything approaching the speed and accuracy of the human brain. But that recall happens ultraconsciously and, Schooler found, can also be disrupted by verbalization. Asking subjects to talk about the process of recalling a face reduced their abilities by up to 50 percent.[105]

Schooler and his fellow researchers coined the term "verbal overshadowing" to describe the phenomenon of conscious, verbal disruption of non-conscious activities. "Metaphorically speaking," he wrote, "verbalization may cause such a ruckus in the 'front' of one's mind that one is unable to attend to the new approaches that may be emerging in the 'back' of one's mind."[106]

The Pains of Thinking. In a "Far Side" cartoon by Gary Larson, we see a bespectacled man looking at a bookshelf. Flames and a horned demon in the background make obvious the cartoon's caption: "Hell's library." And what's on the shelves? Math books. Specifically, "Story Problems," "Big Book of Story Problems," "Story Problems Vol. 3," and of course, "Even More Story Problems."[107] Math, as Larson and many of his fans would agree, is so unpleasant it's comparable to the worst punishments of the eternally damned.

Most of us don't like story problems. We don't like memorizing and studying. We have to force our children to go to school and do their homework. We have at least 100 billion brain cells, and we'd rather keep as many of them idle as possible, at least for conscious processing.

Thinking hurts! Memorization, concentration and complex problem solving are just plain unpleasant for most of us. Indeed, most of us would rather impair our conscious functioning with the help of alcohol and the like than use our brains on something difficult.

It doesn't have to be that way. Evolution alone decides what is pleasurable and what is painful. A little salt on your tongue tastes good because mammalian bodies need salt and mammals therefore evolved the trait long ago to like it. But salt on a slug damages the slug's outer membrane, so the slug avoids it like fire.

Strychnine, like many other things that are bad for you, tastes bitter. If it were good for you, your ancestors would long ago have evolved to find it sweet.

The darkness frightens us not because there's anything inherently wrong with the absence of light. Many creatures prefer the night. But for humans, darkness brings dangers, and thus our minds evolved to find it unpleasant.

We like fat, sugar and making love because those born with the preference for such things found favor long ago in the fight for genetic survival.

And if concentration were good for us, we would like that too. But it was not. Too much conscious thinking, we may conclude, interfered with the calculations and instructions of the ultraconscious and led to death and reproductive failure. Those who found thinking unpleasant and painful prevailed. They're the ones who survived and had children and became your parents.

There's nothing inherently wrong with thinking, mind you. Your brain's doing a ton of it right now, trillions or quadrillions of operations worth of thought every second, and that doesn't hurt at all. But keep your conscious focused on simple things. Think about your next meal or your next sex act, or someone you hate. Just don't think too hard. Your ultraconscious will do the heavy intellectual lifting, and he'll let you know when he's reached a decision and what you should do about it.

Pascal Boyer compares the decision-making process among various parts of the brain to a group of people trying to issue a ruling in a legal case:

> . . . mental systems do not present their evidence in front of a mental judge or jury. They decide the case even before it is presented to any other system. Indeed, many mental systems do not even bother to present a coherent and unified brief. They just send bits of evidence to other systems, presenting them as fact rather than in the form of an argued brief.[108]

Notes Boyer, ". . . we sometimes weigh evidence and decide on its merit. On the other hand, there seems to be a great deal of underground beliefmaking going on that is simply not reported."[109]

The Difficulties of Thinking. Even if thinking didn't hurt, it's just plain hard for a variety of reasons.

First of all, it's exhausting. You're allowed a little concentration now and then, should you want it, but soon enough, your brain will start to shut down. Witness life on a college campus during final exams, when students must spend hours at a time concentrating and memorizing. After a time, the mind rebels, leading to giddiness, pranks and something akin to hysteria. One of my college classmates and I spent several final exam nights slipping lit firecrackers under our friends' bedroom doors.

Again, it doesn't have to be this way. The cells of your ultraconscious never rest, even during a coma. So the conscious neurons should be able to do the same thing. But even during less strenuous bouts of concentration, the mind is constantly subject to daydreaming and distraction – food, frustration, hope, fantasy, sex. And in the event something causes strong emotion – a fight, romance, great fortune or great bad luck – deep thinking goes entirely to sleep.

Conscious thinking hurts, it's difficult and we often get things wrong, limiting our individual ability to challenge the ultraconscious.

So what happens when you encounter someone else's intelligence? How will your ultraconscious react when he perceives someone else in possession of logical and calculative abilities that challenge his supremacy? He won't like it, of course. And therefore, neither will you.

The Social Opposition to Thinking. One of the oddest experiences of my professional life occurred when I was the education reporter for the *Savannah News-Press* in Georgia from 1990 to 1992. Among the institutions I wrote about were the public school system, several state colleges and Savannah College of Art and Design.

For some reason I never quite understood, the husband and wife who founded SCAD in 1978 had adopted a siege mentality in which they perceived hordes of enemies among the local populace and their own students and employees.

They fought with the city and neighboring businesses over zoning matters. They sued a competing art school. They fired staff and tenured faculty at will, earning a rare censure from the American Association of University Professors.[110] They fought with my newspaper, never in the two years I covered the school responding to a single request from me for information or a comment on any matter. They even, for unknown reasons, had secret photographs taken of me and a fellow reporter.

The school's dictatorial policies eventually sparked a campus-wide crisis in the spring of 1992. Students, faculty and board members rose up to question the way the school was being run.

And the family who ran the school, assisted by their loyal administrators, dealt ruthlessly with each group in turn.

When a group of professors attempted to form a faculty senate that spring, the school fired most of them without even the illusion of due process. When several members of the SCAD Board of Trustees raised questions about the goings on, the college removed them (including nationally-known writer Joyce Maynard). When a handful of graduate students attempted to organize a student government, they were accused by school officials of involvement in a small explosion near a college building. Although the students had solid alibis (and two other students not connected to the movement were eventually convicted of that and several other explosions), they were not allowed to register for the next semester and most eventually transferred to other art schools.

Remember, this was just an art college. But with its paranoid and autocratic administration, it might just as easily have been a police state. There was secrecy, spying (one employee told me she caught her boss peering in at her from a fire escape), an aura of fear, and summary terminations – of those suspected of disloyalty – carried out with the speed and efficiency of a ruthless dictatorship.

And, as in a dictatorship, the ones forced out at SCAD were often the most thoughtful ones, the students and faculty who dared to question, who proposed better ways of doing things and had the courage and imagination to call publicly for improvements.

I continue to believe that the ousted students represented the best of SCAD's student body. They organized large, well-run meetings and rallies. When college administrators cancelled that spring's graduation under the flimsy excuse that they feared another explosion, the leaders of the student movement worked with dissident faculty to conduct their own graduation ceremony. More than 1,000 people came to the event, a moving tribute both to academic achievement and to the honor of struggling against misguided authority.

Ultimately, I witnessed firsthand a drama that I believe has been played out many, many times through human history. Evolution favors the powerful in a group because they typically receive more resources and more mating opportunities, so the pursuit of power is very likely an evolved trait. Clinging to power by any means necessary is also an evolved trait, we may logically assume, and history is awash with examples of powerful humans resorting to utter barbarism for the sake of staying in control, including the torturing and execution of anyone who challenges their rule.

So who were those potentates killing? The same sorts of people kicked out at SCAD, surely. The thoughtful, the imaginative, the creative.

The intelligent.

History is rife with instances of intelligence as a capital crime. Both Stalin and Hitler targeted what were called the Intelligentsia during their reigns. Thousands of Europe's most educated and most thoughtful, including writers, poets and scientists, were imprisoned and killed. The Khmer Rouge, who killed at least a million people in Cambodia, focused their genocidal energies on the educated and intelligent as well. The mere wearing of glasses got many people executed. Today, where there are political prisoners (and there are still many, sadly), they are often the most literate, the most educated, and therefore the greatest threat to the manufactured realities of today's ultraconscious-driven tyrants.

We humans may believe we are smart, and credit the evolutionary forces that always favored the smartest among us, but I challenge that idea here. It is conscious stupidity that evolution favors, I believe, not just forced on us by our own minds to keep us from interfering with our ultraconsciouses, but for similar reasons reinforced, encouraged and rewarded in aggregate by human cultures around the world and throughout history.

If your intelligence is dangerous to your own ultraconscious, so is the intelligence of others, proposing as they might new ideas that challenge the illusions your ultraconscious has gone to so much trouble to create for you.

Long ago, the Bible offered scriptural justification for the resistance to intelligence, warning, "For in much wisdom is much grief; and he that increaseth knowledge increaseth sorrow." (Ecclesiastes 1:18)

The social and evolutionary dynamics that maintain conscious stupidity are indeed so powerful, apparently, that – millennia after we began leaving the jungle behind – the ancient dramas recur everywhere, even in an art school in a beautiful city.

A few pages ago, I listed some of the more common words we use for the stupid. But we also maintain a varied vocabulary of insults for those who are intelligent: Egghead, poindexter, bookworm, geek, know-it-all, longhair, dweeb, nerd, pointy head, overachiever, elitist etc.

Few of us want to be called such things. The modern world, with all its wonders, conveniences and discoveries, may have been built by such people, but we don't have to admire, like, date or marry them. And have children with them? Absolutely not! Please, let the genes of the brilliant die with them. Let intelligence wither and fade wherever it appears. The ultraconscious doesn't need it and doesn't want it.

If superior cognition were a desirable trait, the most intelligent among us would be the most attractive. Children at recess would quiz each other on math and spelling, with those best at the competition always the most popular. Young men and women would vie for inclusion on the debating and chess teams, dating each other to the exclusion of the rest.

But of course the opposite is true. Even in an era where lifespan has been doubled through the determined, systematic application of cognition, individuals who possess superior mental powers are characterized as unattractive, undesirable, even sinister. Literature and drama return constantly to the theme of great intelligence gone awry, leading to unintended tragedy or to schemes of world-ending evil.

In one of countless literary examples I might cite of wayward brilliance, I turn to "The Birth-Mark," a short story I read in high school and found poignant. Written by Nathaniel Hawthorne and first published in 1843, it featured a brilliant scientist, Aylmer, and his obsession with the small birthmark on the face of his otherwise perfectly beautiful wife, Georgiana. Aylmer tries various cures for getting rid of the birthmark, finally succeeding with a potion that also kills her.

Analyses of the story's theme and meaning typically focus on man's futile quest for perfection, or the complexities of sexuality between the spouses. But there is another glaring theme: intelligence and the inventions it spawns can kill (and note that Aylmer killed his mate before they'd had any children, a significant detail in this context).

Is that what Hawthorne wanted us to take away from the story? We'll never be sure, but I would guess not – the theme of destructive, murderous brilliance is so universal, so accepted that it stands on its own, a literary vehicle for other, less obvious messages.

Aylmer was not evil, but many of literature's brightest are. The expression "evil genius" has entered common usage in English. There's even a pop song by that title.[111] In film and TV, the very smart are often presented as fundamentally flawed, morally or physically or both. They are crippled, wheelchair-bound, deformed – unworthy of love, incapable of sex.

Examples abound in literature and drama, particularly in more recent times as conscious intelligence began to come into its own. A few instances from the most popular current fiction, some benign, some evil:

> **Albus Dumbledore.** The wise headmaster of Hogwarts in the popular *Harry Potter* series is imagined by the books' creator, J.K. Rowling, to be "quite asexual. He led a celibate and a bookish life."[112]

Currently one of the most popular fiction writers, Dan Brown regularly relies on such characters. **Maximilian Kohler,** the brilliant physicist, director of the European Organization for Nuclear Research (CERN) in Brown's *Angels & Demons*, requires a wheelchair and is weak and infirm. **Sir Leigh Teabing,** the clever historian and scholar in *The Da Vinci Code*, is childless and loveless, his only companion a male butler who ultimately betrays him. He walks with the aid of crutches due to a bout of polio earlier in life. **Mal'akh,** the villain who continuously outwits the CIA in *The Lost Symbol*, castrates himself.

Frankenstein. In the 1818 book by Mary Shelley, the hulking, murderous monster is the creation and namesake of the brilliant Dr. Victor Frankenstein.

Aliens. Fictional otherworldly visitors to earth, whose superior intelligence may be taken for granted, are rarely presented attractively in books and movies. They have big, hairless heads (often shaped like giant brains, interestingly), black eyes and reptilian skin. And they're usually here to kill us.

Comic Book Villains. The bad guys are brilliant and fantastically inventive, able to create diabolical killing contraptions and earth-destroying weaponry. They are often also ugly, crippled or otherwise poor choices for mates.

Atlantis. While it was merely an evil empire in Plato's fictional account, the lost continent of Atlantis exists in modern fiction and imagination as a place destroyed by its own brilliant technology.

Prometheus. For the crime of bringing the knowledge of fire to man, this tragic demigod of Greek legend was chained to rocks and had his perpetually-regenerating liver devoured each day by an eagle. The gods of old, it seems, were just as opposed to human knowledge as the ultraconscious is today.

The Tree of Knowledge. The creation myth that begins the Bible and is claimed by all of the Abrahamic faiths centers on what is known as the Tree of the Knowledge of Good and Evil. Significantly, its name is often shortened in modern references to the Tree of Knowledge, and the decision by the first humans, Adam and Eve, to eat its fruit condemned all humanity to difficult lives that ended in death.

Why does the story of destructive, tragic and barren wisdom and brilliance keep recurring? Have authors, mythicists, movie producers and comic book artists united in a vast conspiracy to make us think all greatly intelligent people are destructive, doomed, sinister and, worst of all, not marriageable?

No, far more likely is that depictions of fictional intelligence, like fictional love, war, good and evil, represent what humans –

around the world and through history – find most compelling. An author imagines a story and commits it to paper only if it appeals to her personally. Then it is presented to others, and only those stories which appeal universally live on.

Only those stories, that is, that appeal universally to the ultraconscious live on. Remember, most of what you like and don't like – friends, lovers, music, religion, houses, jobs etc. – are not chosen by your rational conscious, but instead selected in secret by your ultraconscious. The same goes for your taste in stories about smart people.

Which would you rather read, a book about a brilliant astrophysicist who is so attractive he or she is constantly propositioned, or a book about the same astrophysicist who lives alone, suffers from some disability and is a failure in love? If you prefer the latter, you're in good company. Intelligence, and intelligent people, make your ultraconscious uneasy, so the message about them he sends your conscious is constant and consistent: Don't like them, don't love them, don't listen to their dangerous ideas, and for heaven's sake, don't be one of them!

Scientists "are seen as social misfits, obsessed with arcane matters and lacking the social skills that might land them a date with the prom queen or one of the cheerleaders," observes scientist Hank Davis in *Caveman Logic: The Persistence of Primitive Thinking in a Modern World.* "They seem to understand things that most normal people cannot; that alone makes them objects of fear and mistrust. We need scientists to invent things or keep us safe, but we'd rather not be around them."[113]

Adds Davis, "(T)he simple truth is that average people are fearful of others who are *too smart*. If you tell them that you're a scientist, they look kind of oddly at you. You're no longer one of them."[114]

In 1964, Richard Hofstadter won a non-fiction Pulitzer Prize for his book *Anti-Intellectualism in American Life*, a title that captures the point succinctly. For centuries, Hofstadter asserted, as America was birthed and became a superpower, significant elements of the populace have resisted intelligence, expertise and education in favor of superstition and "common sense."[115]

A similar sentiment is captured in the title of a more recent work, Charles Pierce's *Idiot America: How Stupidity Became a*

Virtue in the Land of the Free. Pierce laments "the breakdown of a consensus that the pursuit of knowledge is a good" and decries the "ascendancy of the notion that the people whom we should trust the least are the people who best know what they're talking about."[116]

In *Caveman Logic*, Davis blames movies and the rest of the entertainment industry for science's bad reputation, writing that "(P)opular culture seems to delight in disdaining those carriers of the scientific method: the scientists, themselves." But I propose here that the well-documented bias against intelligence – in America as well as in the rest of the world – flows from a much deeper place than modern entertainment, that there is an inherent, ultraconscious bias against it that predates Hollywood by perhaps several hundred thousand years.

Too much intelligence threatens our once-essential, ultraconscious conclusions, so our ultraconscious lashes out against it, declaring advanced cognition to be ugly, impotent, demonic. In Italy, they say that "people talk about philosophy and liberty only because they can't get a hard-on."[117] Do not think too hard or tolerate those who do, or you will never reproduce. In fact, you won't even have sex,a because you're impotent.

Indeed, if someone challenges your ideas, call them an idiot and, for good measure, despise them. One of the reasons sensible people refuse to discuss religion or politics is that such discussions often lead to irritation, antagonism, even hatred. In a sense, people with opinions that contradict yours are as dangerous to you as people who are coughing and sneezing. One presents a challenge to your physical integrity, the other a challenge to the integrity of the beliefs your ultraconscious has created for you. Hatred in either case reduces contact and prevents infection.

When society does decide to tolerate intelligence, it often does so in highly proscriptive ways. As cultures adopt an alphabet and begin to emerge as a civilization, heightened intelligence is required among the class of people who must maintain and pass on certain knowledge, particularly written religious knowledge. But these cultures often seem to make a deal with their most intelligent: we'll let you be smart and literate as long as your smart genes die with you.

Time and again, from the scholarly priests of the Catholic Church to the truth-seeking Jain monks of India, celibacy is mandatory. Often, these monks and priests shave their heads, and one might theorize that doing so makes them look older, thus less virile and less attractive to women. Catholic holy men were sometimes shaved only on top of the head, in what was called a tonsure. Whatever its religious rationale, the style looked very like an advanced case of male-pattern balding.

The near-universal deprivation of education for women, at least until the very recent past, deserves acknowledgement in this context.

The justifications for this educational practice, when they are made explicit, are often some variation of religion (God wants it this way), or economics (women's work doesn't require education), or patriarchal (knowledge is for men only), or physiological (e.g. academic pursuits force blood to the brain and away from the uterus, reducing the woman's reproductive potential[118]), but one can't help but speculate on ultraconscious motives.

There is considerable evidence that women are inherently more collaborative than men, less belligerent, more compassionate and nurturing, less selfish and hateful. One might argue that women's brains were designed this way, because such traits are more suitable to the nurturing of children and close cooperation with other women of the clan, while the men were out hunting, competing with each other and killing enemies. So women carry in their minds a constant threat to the ultraconscious' ruthless, evolutionarily-favored (and grossly obsolete) agenda. An educated woman, especially a literate one, with her enhanced abilities to gather information to support her ideas and to speak and write about them, is that much more dangerous.

The evidence for enforced stupidity, against women, or anyone who exhibits intelligence, is as dramatic as the many libraries burned and pillaged through the ages – at Alexandria, Antioch, Ctesiphon, Nalanda, Granada – and as subtle as the snickers when the smartest kid in class gets another answer right.

How Understanding Secret 5 Might Make You Happier

If you are like most people, you have learned to trust your hunches and superstitions, to avoid heavy thinking, to yield without question to your emotions and to be suspicious of too much smarts in others.

Such an approach to life used to work, thus its evolutionary favor, but it is completely out of place in the modern world. And therein lies unhappiness, both for you and the others whose lives you touch.

You have to know things to be happy. Dumb people don't know things. And we're all dumb. 'Nuff said.

The harms of stupidity go well beyond your own welfare. If you reject or ignore science and wallow in evolved stupidity, you are also rejecting that which brings health and happiness to your fellow human beings, your children and your more distant offspring.

Can it be overcome? Of course. Treat your brain like a muscle and exercise it. Read difficult things. Write on occasion. Work puzzles. Talk to someone you disagree with, see if you can use logic to refute her points, and if you can't, do something completely unhuman, utterly unevolved and radically life-changing: acknowledge her persuasiveness and admit that you might be wrong, or at least that you have some more research to do.

Celebrate intelligence. Revere brilliance. If you stop avoiding it, you might find a little in yourself.

A Final Word on Intelligence: Evolving Smarter

We are quite stupid, we humans. And yet, intelligence persists. Somehow, the human conscious has held its own through the long, dark millennia, fighting against overwhelming odds within and without to emerge – in every tenth or hundredth or thousandth person – and do something profound. Brilliance has crawled through the muck of ignorance, superstition and the inherent pains of thought to stand up, now and then, and give the rest of us slightly better, more interesting lives, through the telescope, the printing press, Impressionism, Fifth Symphonies, representative democracy, the steam engine, penicillin, neuroscience, the Theory of Relativity and the internet.

But how much longer will *any* intelligence last? What is to become of humankind if the dumbest among us are no longer weeded out by natural selection? If we permit the unintelligent not only to survive, thanks to the modern contrivances of welfare, medicine and compassion, but to reproduce, aren't we at risk of dumbing down the human race to the point of no return?

Within a generation of Darwin, people began asking this question, and acting on the principles that came to be known as eugenics: the idea that humankind could be improved if we ensured that only the superior produced offspring. The darker corollary occurred to people simultaneously, that we should prevent the reproduction of the inferior for the best human destiny.

These ideas, in the hands of racists, the selfish and those gripped by fear and, yes, stupidity, led directly to the slaughter of six million people by the Nazis, many more murders elsewhere, and the forced sterilization of thousands around the world in the first half of the 20th century.

To our credit, humans stepped back from that abyss, driven by a visceral sense that these were very bad things. The question hasn't gone away, however. Is human intelligence doomed if we're not actively weeding out the least intelligent?

The 2006 movie *Idiocracy* proposes a comedic "yes" to the question – within 500 years, humans will have evolved to become so stupid they'll destroy their crops by watering them with a sports drink called Brawndo.

Based on the ideas of this chapter, I would propose an entirely different outcome. Modern life isn't enabling the reproduction of the least fit among us; instead, for the first time in human evolution, intelligence is no longer punishable by death.

We remain ultraconsciously mistrustful of intelligence in ways that our language, fiction and personal choices continue to reinforce, but increasingly, the ability to think up a great idea or two leads not to death but to money, fame, spouses and, most importantly, children.

There are, indeed, well-defined paths toward success and offspring for the intelligent that simply did not exist until the last century or two. There are school loans, academic prizes and scholarships to enable the most intelligent to increase their knowledge. There are copyrights and patents and intellectual property laws that enable the brilliant to protect the ability of their ideas to make money for them. And there is a free press and a worldwide network of media that recognize and applaud the creators of the best ideas, granting them the respect, renown and sexual attractiveness that was – in all previous eras – reserved for the best fighters and hunters.

The human race, for all its stupidity, for its sad, endless history of wars and ignorance and waste, has at last won the right to be intelligent.

On a more personal note, so have you. Surrounded by anti-intellectualism both subtle and blatant, you no longer need to fear the intelligence you encounter in yourself or others. The embrace of knowledge and reason, so critical to the pursuit of happiness, is no longer a capital crime. You are free in a way no humans have ever been before.

Secret 6: Your Ultraconscious Can't Protect You from Exploitation

I'll start this chapter with a simple summary:

There are little evolved, obsolete buttons all over your brain that other people can push to make you do things that are good for them and bad for you. And until you know what each button does, and can train yourself to resist when someone else pushes it, you cannot call yourself free, powerful, or fully conscious.

According to mismatch theory, discussed in Secret 1, humans evolved in an ancient world very different from the place we occupy now. There was more danger, more brutality, less certainty and less food. It was harder to reproduce, travel or be sure about anything. Only those humans whose brains were most finely tuned for life in such a place could hope to make it from day to day. While the conscious was valuable for certain operations, there would still need to be plenty of automatic behaviors. An instant, ultraconscious response to a hurtling object could make the difference between life and death, for example. Indeed, the ability for rapid-fire, unquestioning reactions to any number of stimuli determined, long ago, who would live and have children and who would perish without descendants.

Imagine for a moment, if you will, that the average human is rather like a toy called "Busy Poppin' Pals," which I found advertised at the Playskool website in early 2011. The toy is covered with buttons the child can "slide, push, press, turn and click." The manipulation of each button results in a "friendly animal face that bursts out of its colored, numbered box."

In the same way, the manipulation of various buttons on the human psyche results in behaviors that are sometimes disconcertingly like those animal faces. Throw something at a human, insult one, stare at one, scream, trip or smile, and the reactions are almost as predictable as what happens when you play with Busy Poppin' Pals.

The fact is, people the world over react the same way to the same things, even if doing so hurts them, causes pain, costs money or gets others upset with them. Unfortunately, some of these automatic behaviors also can result in good things for other people, and in due time an entire subclass of human beings has arisen that makes its living off exploiting your evolved, automatic vulnerabilities. These exploiters are not much different from a child playing with Busy Poppin' Pals. Declared the website, "Figuring out which way to move, click, push or twist each button on the Busy Poppin' Pals requires a little luck, some trial and error and good problem-solving skills!"

Change a few words and you have described one of the grimmest aspects of the human condition: "Figuring out which way to provoke, frighten, deceive or otherwise exploit the evolved stimulus-response reflexes of your fellow humans requires a little luck, some trial and error and good problem-solving skills!"

Your ultraconscious is as stuck in his ways as a plastic toy. He hasn't noticed yet that you're living in the modern world, so when something happens that required a certain response in the jungle or on the savanna, he'll insist on that same response now.

You can disagree with him, however. Indeed, refusing to allow your buttons to be pressed and levers to be slid is about more than protecting yourself; it is in fact a crucial obligation, a moral imperative. Each time you allow your ancient, evolved responses to be manipulated by a clever modern practitioner, you hand over your pursuit of happiness to someone who has no concern for you. Worse, you reward that practitioner with your money and support, ensuring that he'll keep doing it – to you, to others, and eventually to your children and grandchildren.

Religion is fertile ground for your exploitation. For reasons touched on a few secrets ago, our brains are programmed to believe the supernatural, and long ago, people realized they could exploit the superstitious inclinations of their fellows by making up plausible religions – thereby winning money, fame, sex and power.

"Religion," said Seneca, the Roman philosopher, "is regarded by the common people as true, by the wise as false, and by rulers as useful."

The human inclination to gamble, to take risks for possible rewards, is a second button that's easy to exploit on many of us. We are the descendants of risk takers, of people who ventured into unknown lands, who won fights to the death for a better place to live, who got so good at hunting that even the biggest, most dangerous beasts were wiped out across whole continents. Today, that evolved impulse to gamble means more than $100 billion in worldwide revenue from casinos alone in 2010.[119] The universal understanding that the house always wins does not dissuade millions of people from venturing their hard-earned salaries, their inheritances and other people's money on a chance. The house, for its part, is only too happy to oblige.

Along with the evolved willingness to take risks, we are also drawn to gambling thanks to our misplaced confidence in our ability to predict what's going to happen next in a given situation. Life and death depended during our formative eons on being able to guess the next behavior – of an animal, a person, the weather – based on past behavior, so we evolved to get good at it and to trust our judgment. Gambling machines, on the other hand, are "designed to deliver events independently of their history," notes Steven Pinker, and thus to "defeat our intuitive predictions."[120]

We might imagine your ultraconscious rubbing his figurative hands together when he learns that the casino down the road has just made someone a millionaire. "Trust me," he says to you, "we'll be next. I know how things work, and I can predict anything. Let's go!"

Gambling is as old as human behavior, and many have fallen victim. Our exploitation seems unlikely to end, furthermore, despite the remarkable strides we have made in many realms. Indeed, modern technology is being used to make the most of our weaknesses. A chilling passage appears in the *New Yorker* magazine from March 2012, describing a software system designed for a casino by a company called Tibco. The technology, the article reads, "can figure out when a gambler is about to encounter a loss of such magnitude that it will cause him to leave the casino and perhaps never come back. The casino's Luck Ambassadors will then offer the gambler a free meal or a ticket to a show . . . and distract the gambler long enough to entice him to return later, to continue losing money in palatable increments."[121]

While exploitation comes in many forms, and some interesting things could be written here about the ways that the tobacco industry engineers its product to maximize addiction, I will focus on a vocation I began practicing after I got my MBA and left the newspaper business behind in 1994: Marketing.

"Anything too stupid to be said is sung," said Voltaire, the 18th century French writer and humanist. He was referring most likely to the average love ballad which, if it weren't sung, didn't rhyme and were reduced to a series of prosaic sentences, would sound ridiculous.

So would the average advertisement. It is not the job of marketers to say sensible things, employ logic or write excellent prose. It is their job to get your money from you, and a principle strategy is promising happiness, regardless what they're selling – particularly if what they're selling has no direct connection to any real benefit. "Have a Coke and a smile," suggested ads for the soft drink in 1979. In 2008, Pepsi introduced a new logo that featured a suspiciously smile-like set of curves. A 2011 campaign for Coke made the connection between its product and joy even more explicit, stating simply, "open happiness."

Advertisements for soft drinks, alcohol and cigarettes invariably show happy people consuming the product. And that's it: Happy people ingest, inhale and imbibe our stuff. An ad campaign that admitted that the promoted product sometimes caused weight gain, diabetes, lung cancer, addiction, divorce and job loss would be unthinkable, but far more honest.

Every smiling advertisement is a lie. In the ancient world where we evolved, a smiling face meant something precious: a friend, a family member, a lover, someone who would share something essential to our reproductive success. A smile indicated that the person was happy and thus whatever they were doing was good and could make us happy too. Today, we are bombarded with the smiles of people who have been paid to smile, but our naïve, evolved brains still connect instantly the smile to whatever's being sold. We forget or ignore that we are being manipulated, convince ourselves happiness is certain (so desperate are we always for happiness) if only we can do that thing the other person is doing, and we work to earn money to make liars rich.

"Show a bright side, the happy and attractive side, not the dark and uninviting side of things," recommended Claude Hopkins in *Scientific Advertising*, the 1923 book that is still considered the bible of marketing wisdom and experience.

Hopkins said the advice he dispensed in his book was all based on extensive trials, where the sole objective was to see what techniques most effectively got people to part with their money:

> We learn the principles and prove them by repeated tests. This is done through keyed advertising, by traced returns, largely by the use of coupons. We compare one way with many others, backward and forward and record the results. When one method invariably proves the best, that method becomes a fixed principle . . . One ad is compared with another, one method with another. Headlines, settings, sizes, arguments and pictures are compared . . . (N)o guesswork is permitted. One must know what is best.[122]

Through such a process of trial and error, understanding human psychology isn't necessary. Regardless what weakness, vulnerability or superstition is being exploited, all that matters is that it worked by generating income for the advertiser.

Some marketing messages go straight to the brain without any need for conscious permission. A cookie retailer is known to vent the steam from its ovens into the malls where it operates, creating an irresistible aroma. Christmas music is played in shopping centers as early as Halloween to make people want to buy gifts.

Given its central role in evolution, sex has also proven to be a powerful marketing force. "Our advertising appeals are permeated with erotic references," writes Jeremy Rifkin in *The Empathic Civilization*, noting that psychologists, inspired by Freud's fixation with sexual motivations, have been making money with sex-based marketing for more than a century. "Much of the success of consumer capitalism over the course of the past century is due, in no small part, to the eroticization of desires and the sexualization of consumption."[123]

Not all advertising is allowed to be completely positive. In pharmaceutical advertising, the side effects and risks of the advertised product must by law be revealed. But clever marketers have gotten around that.

Ruth Day, director of the Medical Cognition Laboratory at Duke University, has documented in numerous studies that viewers of advertisements for prescription drugs tend to forget the adverse side effects mentioned in the ads.[124] What's going on? One marketing technique she spotted is the introduction of distracting sounds and images while negative information is being presented.

For example, Day reported in one hearing on the topic, "the bee in the Nasonex TV commercial beat its wings furiously when risk information was being presented but was still when benefit information was presented."[125]

As insidious as exploiting you for money is, more worrisome perhaps are recent trends in political marketing.

Consistently over the last few decades, one percent of Americans have controlled about one-third of the nation's wealth, and their use of new communication technologies for the ever more effective dissemination of political marketing and propaganda, as well as the support of candidates and issues that serve their financial purposes, represent what might end up being a revolutionary power transfer, from the branches of elective government to de facto governance by a rich minority of Americans.

There are countless examples where firms, lobbyists and industry groups pursue profit through propaganda, but Koch Industries stands out. Billionaire brothers David and Charles Koch (pronounced "Coke") have turned to the dissemination of skewed science and carefully-crafted political propaganda to ensure their conglomerate's ongoing ability to pollute profitably.

Selling everything from paper towels to tolulene, the Koch empire was listed in a 2010 report as the tenth biggest polluter in the United States, with 33 million pounds annually of toxic air emissions[126]. Says Greenpeace USA, in a March 2010 report:

> Although Koch intentionally stays out of the public
> eye, it . . . has become a financial kingpin of climate

science denial and clean energy opposition. This private, out-of-sight corporation is now a partner to ExxonMobil, the American Petroleum Institute and other donors that support organizations and front-groups opposing progressive clean energy and climate policy. From 2005 to 2008, ExxonMobil spent $8.9 million while the Koch Industries-controlled foundations contributed $24.9 million in funding to organizations of the 'climate denial machine'. . . . The company's tight knit network of lobbyists, former executives and organizations has created a forceful stream of misinformation that Koch-funded entities produce and disseminate.[127]

Koch and many firms like it disguise their corporate interests behind a mask of ultraconscious triggers, including appeals to nationalism (our tribe is better than their tribe), freedom (our tribe can go anywhere and do whatever we want) and prosperity (our tribe has more stuff than their tribe). All three triggers appear in this paragraph from the firm's website:

For more than 40 years, Koch companies and the Koch foundations have been committed to liberty and free-market principles, which are the foundation of the U.S. Constitution. History demonstrates that greater economic freedom in a society not only fosters advances in innovation, productivity and prosperity, but in environmental protection and quality of life.[128]

Rationalizations for low taxes and minimal environmental regulation are not always put so delicately, of course. Confesses an anonymous political consultant creating ads for the anti-tax Tea Party movement (also heavily funded by the Koch brothers[129]): "We're playing to the reptilian brain rather than the logic centers, so we look for key words and images to leverage the intense rage and anxiety of white working-class conservatives. In other words, I talk to the same part of your brain that causes road rage."[130]

Your exploitation through such political machinations is less direct than a marketer enticing you to buy their product, but ultimately may be far more harmful to you. Chemical and energy firms, food producers, pharmaceuticals and gun manufactures can poison your water, pollute your air, put assault weapons in the hands of madmen, corrupt your food and medicine and change the earth's ecological balance – not just make you poorer.

To ensure the longest, happiest life, you must look at any request – to believe a certain way, vote for a certain candidate, give money to a certain cause – with the height of suspicion, particularly when you sense the tug on one of your ancient emotional triggers.

How Understanding Secret 6 Might Make You Happier

Your ultraconscious, helpful as he may be in some areas, cannot protect you from the kinds of exploitation that have emerged in the modern world, the carefully-crafted psychological marketing, the appeals to your superstition, the wealth- and technology-driven business propaganda. Indeed, because your ultraconscious doesn't know what he doesn't know, he colludes against your own best interests with those who want only to get your money or your misguided support.

How can you protect yourself? The trick is to identify the areas of your life where exploitation is taking place – no small feat, unfortunately. As described elsewhere in this book, your own brain is lying to you, your intelligence is severely limited, and you are evolved to be emotional, superstitious, and illogical. But if you are to escape the fate of the animal faces affixed to "Busy Poppin' Pals," whose appearance occurs invariably when certain buttons or levers are pressed, you have no choice but to apply fact and logic to every important decision you make.

Secret 7: You're in Charge, Regardless What Your Ultraconscious Tells You

There is no more powerful, insidious, destructive, beneficial presence in your life – or the history of humanity – than the ultraconscious. He is the counter, the rememberer, the mathematician. He is the sage, the prophet, the power behind the throne. He is looking out for you, keeping you alive and breeding.

But that doesn't mean he cares about your happiness. He wants victory, a victory programmed into the first genes of planet earth – and all genes since – to be defined in one way: successful replication.

Outrageously powerful but fantastically secretive, it has taken more than 100,000 years, and thousands of scientists, experimenters, test subjects and technologies, for humankind to identify this most central aspect of its personality. We have only scratched the surface, and this brief book is but a sliver of all we know. I'd like to think that it's an important sliver, though, focused as it is on your happiness.

But what do you do now? How do you pursue happiness with a brain that's stupid by design and occupied by an invisible being who lies to you, doesn't care about your happiness and – despite all his intelligence – can't protect you from falling into other people's traps?

You can't yell at him; he won't hear you. You can't evict him; you need him far too much. You can't argue with him; he doesn't speak your language.

But you can know about him, and in knowing, there is vast power. Mere knowledge is the force that unlocked the atom, created the computer and put humans on the moon. Now this power has been turned inward by humankind, to unlock the mysteries of the human essence. Our generation is the first to explore this ultimate frontier, and every day we push further.

Knowing he's there, knowing the reasons he does what he does – and knowing that you can still have happiness despite him – gives you a power beyond anything even the wisest of humans possessed in any other age.

Still, there is much to learn. "For now, this is the state of evolutionary psychology:" Robert Wright lamented, "so much fertile terrain, so few farmers."[131]

As incomplete as our knowledge is today, however, we know more than enough to look to it for guidance. To that end, the following might be helpful:

The 7 Commandments of Happiness Your Brain Doesn't Want You to Know

1. **Do not believe everything you believe.** Your brain is a magician, a hypnotist, an illusionist, a false prophet and, in one word, a liar. The bigger the decision, the more facts you must gather and the more logic you must employ. When you are in conflict with another, particularly, and when your emotions are especially strong, question everything you think you know.

2. **Pursue Happiness Incrementally.** Beware the pursuit or achievement of great leaps in your quality of life. They will be exhilarating, but they will also be stressful and disorienting and might generate an overwhelming, painful ultraconscious backlash.

3. **Enjoy the Small Things.** Food, rest, good conversation, a little sunlight, a pleasant view. These evolved long ago to be keys to happiness, and they will continue to be until we evolve past them – if we ever do. On the other hand, while we evolved long ago to pursue unlimited fame, power and wealth, we so rarely achieved them that we never evolved the ability to enjoy them, or even do much else but use them to screw everything up.

4. **Avoid Superstition.** Avoid especially the organized form of superstition known as religion. As beneficial as faith can be at times, it is based on lies and delusions and possesses an inherent toxicity that is no friend to happiness.

5. **Embrace the Truth.** Celebrate knowledge, logic and intelligence, as frightening as you might find them. The alternative is conscious stupidity and ultraconscious decision-making, both dangerously obsolete in the modern world.

6. **Beware exploitation.** Look past the smiles, the mysticism, the rage-inducing claims and the psychological button-pushing and see instead the motivations behind the requests for your money, your votes, your support and your reverence. To do otherwise is not only to reward your exploiters, but to give them the power and money they need to do it again to your children.

7. **Insist on Overcoming.** Fight the negative elements of your ultraconscious, his lies, the superstition and stupidity he imposes, the vulnerabilities to others he blithely enables. Resisting him is not only a right, but a moral obligation. You are best served by your own effectiveness and awareness. So is the rest of the human race.

Considering what you're up against, overcoming alone might be impossible. Your mind itself is set up to blind you to the happiness failures it imposes. Seeing others' happiness failures is typically far easier, and psychologists and other licensed professionals can be extremely helpful to that end. So too can be the support of peers, armed with the awareness of the many ways the happiness of another might be under assault from within. Mutual support groups are very effective at helping addicts recover. Mutual support groups formed to identify and fight other obstacles to happiness, now that they have been uncovered by science, might be just as productive. New technologies – email, chatrooms, online forums and virtual reality – offer intriguing new avenues to collaboration among those seeking help in the fight against the enemy that lives in our minds.

You are the owner of trillions of cells dedicated only to helping you make your way. You are the owner of a conscious that enables happiness. And now I hope, to the degree this book is true and understandable, you know some of the limits and barriers of that happiness, and some of the ways to get around those limits. You have learned a little about cheating the system for your own joy.

We modern humans are a new species perhaps, more aware of ourselves as creatures of happiness, more knowledgeable about the pursuit of happiness, and more concerned about the happiness of others, than any humans before. Should we invent a new name for ourselves? Homo ebullient? Homo ecstatic? Or is the speciation of modern humankind so dramatic we may call ourselves "hetero," or "different" now? Homo hetero eudaimonia?

"Know thyself," said the Greek Oracle at Delphi. The words, passed down through the millennia as an essential step to enlightenment, have never been closer to fulfillment than they are today.

Good luck.

Epilogue: Yes, This is Revolution

As has probably become obvious by now, this book is about far more than your personal happiness. Ultimately, this book and those like it are revolution, manifestos, new philosophies against the tyrant that has controlled humankind and all the life before and around us, for better and for worse, always.

Indeed, we are in the midst of not just *a* revolution, but perhaps *the* revolution, that singular moment in the four billion year history of life on earth when one of its creatures finally understands what it is – where it came from, why it does what it does, and what must be done next.

This is not what evolution intended. Humans were supposed to get just enough conscious smarts to do whatever it was the ultraconscious needed from us – speak, perhaps; or figure out the basic causes and effects of things the ultraconscious found foreign; or make the final decision when the ultraconscious got stuck on a problem. Who knows? The fact is that the human conscious, thanks to what little intelligence it was allowed, has at last broken free, inventing a world in which its invisible but vastly superior partner has been rendered, in many ways, obsolete.

"As an unexpected bonus," writes Richard Dawkins, "our brains turn out to be powerful enough to accommodate a much richer world model than the mediocre utilitarian one that our ancestors needed in order to survive. Art and science are runaway manifestations of this bonus."[132]

But we're not out of the woods yet. Stupidity remains a powerful voice in human affairs, forcing the conscious to make way for superstition, hunch and passion in matters small, large and existentially grave. We might yet destroy ourselves. And even if we ultimately prevail, stupidity and religion and the lies that come from within continue to throw up grievous impediments, slowing progress, denying fact and logic and, quite literally, killing.

We might continue on the long march toward wisdom, compassion and sustainability, or we might yet bomb or pollute or consume our way back to the Stone Age, if not oblivion.

Evolution, who conjured life from the muck four billion years ago and has ruled iron-fisted over our progress ever since, didn't intend to make beings with the ability to short circuit the basic laws of their own formation. But that's what has happened. Through medicine, science, logic and compassion, we are improving on our physical design, out-thinking the ultraconscious, and feeling a concern for others that violates the most basic principles of survival and reproduction.

"(I)t is perfectly possible to hold that genes exert a statistical influence on human behavior while at the same time believing that this influence can be modified, overridden or reversed by other influences,"[133] Dawkins asserts. "We, alone on earth, can rebel against the tyranny of the selfish replication."[134]

Stephen Pinker, noting that his single and childless life isn't what evolution had mapped out for his genes, put it this way: "(I)f my genes don't like it, they can go jump in the lake."[135]

For better or for worse, we are on our own now. Evolution has held us long enough. We are forcing her fingers apart, taking charge of our destiny, placing our fate in our own hands, which have grown giant. Perhaps we will fly, or perhaps we will drop like a stone.

Evolution was a cruel cage, but it was also a safe cage. "Do exactly as I say and you will live," evolution said to life. After billions of years on planet earth, life has risen up on two legs, learned to speak, and said simply, "No."

END

Acknowledgments

I have been working on versions and variations of this book for what feels like eons, and as I finished each new endeavor, I would present it first to Michelle Andra, a clinical psychologist who also happens to be my wife. Her patience, perseverance and gentle input have added immeasurably to this effort. I also owe a tremendous debt of gratitude to anthropologist Jerome "Jerry" Barkow, who offered helpful feedback and inspiring encouragement on the early chapters of this book. Additional thanks to my editor, Beth Jusino, and the many friends who have taken a look at this or earlier incarnations, including Jean & Richard Miller, Sharon Matchett, Neal Jones, Jackie Campbell and Randall Patterson.

Notes

[1] Nesse, Randolph M. "Natural selection and the elusiveness of happiness." The Royal Society. Published online 31 August 2004. P. 1333.

[2] Widdicombe, Lizzie, "That's Italian," *The New Yorker,* November 2, 2009, p. 44.

[3] Szekely, Louis, aka Louis CK. Conversation on Conan O'Brien, Oct. 3, 2008.

[4] Pinker, Steven. *How the Mind Works.* W. W. Norton & Company. 2009. P. 135.

[5] Boyer, Pascal. *Religion Explained: The Evolutionary Origins of Religions Thought.* Basic Books. 2001. P. 98.

[6] Hendrix, Harville. *Getting the Love You Want: A Guide for Couples.* HarperPerennial (a division of HarperCollins). 1988. p. 8-9.

[7] Pinker, Steven. *How the Mind Works.* W. W. Norton & Company. 2009. P. 135.

[8] Horgan, John. "The Consciousness Conundrum." *IEEE Spectrum.* June 2008. P. 38.

[9] Kurzweil, Ray. *The Age of Spiritual Machines: When Computers Exceed Human Intelligence.* Viking, 1999, Chapter 6.

[10] Logothetis, NK, "The neural basis of the blood-oxygen-level-dependent functional magnetic resonance imaging signal." The Philosophical Transactions of the Royal Society; The Royal Society of London for the Improvement of Natural Knowledge. August 29, 2002. P. 1003-37.

[11] Horovitz SG, Fukunaga M, de Zwart JA, van Gelderen P, Fulton SC, Balkin TJ, Duyn JH. "Low frequency BOLD fluctuations during resting wakefulness and light sleep: a simultaneous EEG-fMRI study." Advanced MRI, LFMI, NINDS, National Institutes of Health, Bethesda, Maryland. June, 2008. P. 671-82.

[12] Owen, Adrian, Coleman, Martin, Boly, Melanie et al, "Detecting Awareness in the Vegetative State," Science, September 8, 2006, Vol. 313. no. 5792, p. 1402.

[13] Shmuel A, Leopold DA. "Neuronal correlates of spontaneous fluctuations in fMRI signals in monkey visual cortex: Implications for functional connectivity at rest." Hum Brain Mapping. July, 2008; P. 751-61.

[14] Hilgard, Ernest R., Atkinson, Richard C., Atkinson, Rita L. "Introduction to Psychology." Sixth Edition. Harcourt Brace Jovanovich, Inc. 1975. p. 176.

[15] Jonah Lehrer, Annals of Science, "The Eureka Hunt," *The New Yorker*, July 28, 2008, p. 40

[16] Klein, Gary. *Sources of Power.* Cambridge: MIT Press. 1998. p. 32.

[17] Wilder, Penfield. "Some Mechanisms of Consciousness Discovered During

Electrical Stimulation of the Brain." Proceedings of the National Academy of Sciences. Volume 44, Number 2, February 15, 1958. p. 60.
[18] Wilder, Penfield. "Some Mechanisms of Consciousness Discovered During Electrical Stimulation of the Brain." Proceedings of the National Academy of Sciences. Volume 44, Number 2, February 15, 1958. p. 58.
[19] Gur, Ruben & Sackeim, Harold. "Self-deception: A concept in search of a phenomenon." *Journal of Personality and Social Psychology,* 1979 37:147–69.
[20] Bechara, Antoine; Damasio, Hanna; Tranel, Daniel; Damasio, Antonio R. "Deciding Advantageously Before Knowing the Advantageous Strategy." Science. Vol. 275. no. 5304. February 28, 1997. p. 1293.
[21] Wittlinger, Matthias, Wehner, Rüdiger, Wolf, Harald. "The Ant Odometer: Stepping on Stilts and Stumps." Science, June 30, 2006, pp. 1965 – 1967.
[22] Bongard, Sylvia and Nieder, Andreas. "Basic mathematical rules are encoded by primate prefrontal cortex neurons." Proceedings of the National Academy of Sciences. Jan. 18, 2010.
[23] Mozes, Alan. "Monkey Brain 'Hardwired' for Simple Math." *HealthDay.* Jan 19. 2010.
[24] Scialdone, Antonio; Mugford, Sam. "Arabidopsis plants perform arithmetic division to prevent starvation at night." eLife;. June 24, 2013. eLife 2013;2:e000669.
[25] Buss, David. "The Evolution of Happiness." *American Psychologist.* January 2000. P. 18.
[26] Grinde, Bjorn. "Happiness in the Perspective of Evolutionary Psychology." *Journal of Happiness Studies* 3: 331–354, 2002. P. 338.
[27] For further reading, I recommend: Le Blanc, Steven; Register, Katherine E. *Constant Battles: The Myth of the Peaceful, Noble Savage.* St. Martin's Press. 2003.
[28] Wright, Robert. *The Moral Animal: Why We Are the Way We Are; The New Science of Evolutionary Psychology.* Vintage Books, 1994. P. 211.
[29] Nesse, Randolph M. "Natural selection and the elusiveness of happiness." The Royal Society. Published online 31 August 2004. P. 1336-37
[30] Nesse, Randolph M. "Natural selection and the elusiveness of happiness." The Royal Society. Published online 31 August 2004. P. 1336-37
[31] Cabanac, Michel. "Emotion and phylogeny" *Japanese Journal of Physiology,* 49. 2009. Pp. 1–10.
[32] Grinde, Bjorn. "Happiness in the Perspective of Evolutionary Psychology." *Journal of Happiness Studies* 3: 331–354, 2002. P. 338.
[33] Wright, Robert. *The Moral Animal: Why We Are the Way We Are; The New Science of Evolutionary Psychology.* Vintage Books, 1994. P. 37.
[34] Meredith, Kevin E. *Heirloom of Agony: A New Theory About Why Happiness Hurts, and What You Can Do About It.* Kevin E Meredith. 2017
[35] Barkow, J. H. (1997). Happiness in Evolutionary Perspective. In N. L. Segal, G. E. Weisfeld & C. C. Weisfeld (Eds.), *Uniting Psychology and Biology. Integrative Perspectives on Human Development.* Washington, DC: American Psychological Association. pp. 397-418.

[36] Jerome H. Barkow, cited elsewhere in this book, deserves credit here for suggesting in a January 2011 email to the author that bipolar disorder might be an example of emotional balancing.

[37] From the biography of Aaron T. Beck, posted at www.beckinstitute.org, January 9, 2010.

[38] Mosby's Medical Dictionary, 8th edition. © 2009, Elsevier.

[39] Damasio, Antonio. *Looking for Spinoza: Joy, Sorrow and the Feeling Brain.* Harcourt. 2003. P. 67-68.

[40] Kasser, Tim. *The High Price of Materialism.* Cambridge: MIT Press, 2002.

[41] Layard, Richard. *Happiness: Lessons From a New Science.* Penguin Press, 2005. p. 48.

[42] Richins, Marsha L. "When Wanting Is Better than Having: Materialism, Transformation Expectations, and Product-Evoked Emotions in the Purchase Process." *Journal of Consumer Research.* Vol. 40, No. 1 (June 2013), pp. 1-18.

[43] Peck, M. Scott. *In Search of Stones.* Simon & Schuster Ltd. 1997. p. 98-99.

[44] Peck, M. Scott. *In Search of Stones.* Simon & Schuster Ltd. 1997. p. 99.

[45] Peck, M. Scott. *In Search of Stones.* Simon & Schuster Ltd. 1997. p. 100.

[46] Sheff, David. "Rock's Bernie Taupin Sings His Own Lyrics Now but He Hasn't Written Elton a Dear John." *People Magazine.* June 23, 1980 Vol. 13 No. 25.

[47]Brickman P., Coates D., Janoff-Bulman, R. "Lottery winners and accident victims: is happiness relative?" *Journal of Personality and Social Psychology.* August, 1978, Volume 36, No. 8. P. 917-27.

[48] Granato, Sherri. "Winning the Lottery, Curse or a Blessing?" October 13, 2006. Posted at: Associated Content, www.associatedcontent.com/article/70165/winning_the_lottery_curse_or_a_blessi ng_pg2.html?cat=47.

[49] Kim, Pilyoung; and Swain, James E. "Sad Dads: Paternal Postpartum Depression." Psychiatry MMC. Volume 4, Issue 2. February 2007. P. 36-47.

[50] Paulson, James F.; Bazemore, Sharnail D. "Prenatal and Postpartum Depression in Fathers and Its Association With Maternal Depression: A Meta-analysis." *The Journal of the American Medical Association.* 303(19). 2010. P. 1961-1969.

[51] WHO Statement. "World Suicide Prevention Day 2008; Around one million people die each year by suicide." September 10, 2008

[52] Twenge, J. M, et al., "Birth cohort increases in psychopathology among young Americans, 1938–2007: A crosstemporal meta-analysis of the MMPI." Clinical Psychology Review. 2010 (doi:10.1016/j.cpr.2009.10.005).

[53] Nesse, Randolph M. & Williams, George C. *Why we get sick.* New York: New York Times Books. 1994. P. 220-221.

[54] Pope Benedict XVI; Seewald, Peter; Taylor, Henry (Translator). "God and the World: A Conversation With Peter Seewald." Ignatius Press. 2000.

[55] Oder, Slawomir. "Why He's a Saint: The Real John Paul II According to the Postulator of His Beatification Cause." 2010.

[56] Sandler, David; Hayes, John. "You Can't Teach a Kid to Ride a Bike at a Seminar." Bayhead Publishing, Inc. 2003. P. 210.

[57] Kubler-Ross, Elizabeth. "On Death & Dying." Simon & Schuster/Touchstone.

1969.

58 Wallis, Claudia. "HAPPINESS: What Makes the Human heart sing? Researchers are taking a close look. What they've found may surprise you." Time. January 17, 2005.

59 Peck, M. Scott. *In Search of Stones.* Simon & Schuster Ltd. 1997. p. 141.

60 Damasio, Antonio. Looking for Spinoza: Joy, Sorrow and the Feeling Brain. Harcourt. 2003. P. 68.

61 Peck, M. Scott. *In Search of Stones.* Simon & Schuster Ltd. 1997. p. 99-100.

62 Peck, M. Scott. *In Search of Stones.* Simon & Schuster Ltd. 1997. p. 100.

63 Taupin, Heather. "Bernard Taupin: Biography." http://www.berniejtaupin.com/biography.bt. Website accessed January 10, 2011.

64 Trivers, Robert. "The elements of a scientific theory of self-deception." Annals of the New York Academy of Sciences, 907. 2000. p. 129.

65 Trivers, Robert. "The elements of a scientific theory of self-deception." Annals of the New York Academy of Sciences, 907. 2000. p. 114.

66 Vedantam, Shankar. *The Hidden Brain.* Spiegel & Grau/The Random House Publishing Group. 2010. p. 21.

67 Burley, Nancy. "The Evolution of Concealed Ovulation." *The American Naturalist.* Vol. 114, No. 6. December 1979. Pp 835.

68 Miller, Geoffrey; Tybur, Joshua M. and Jordan, Brent D. *Evolution and Human Behavior,* Volume 28, Issue 6, November 2007, Pages 375-381.

69 Melzack, R., and Wall, P.D. "Pain mechanisms: a new theory." Science 150, 1965. Pages 971-79.

70 Melzack, R., and Wall, P.D. "This Week's Citation Classic." Current Contents Institute for Scientific Information, Number 23, June 7, 1982. Page 22.

71 Ramachandran, VS; Rogers-Ramachandran, D. "Synaesthesia in phantom limbs induced with mirrors." *Proceedings of the Royal Society - Biological Sciences.* April 1996. **263** (1369). Pp. 377–86.

72 Tilburt, Jon C.; Emanuel, Ezekiel J.; Kaptchuk, Ted J.; Curlin, Farr A.; Miller, Franklin G. "Prescribing 'placebo treatments': results of national survey of US internists and rheumatologists." BMJ (formerly the British Medical Journal) October 23, 2008, BMJ 2008;337:a1938.

73 Hrobjartsson, Asbjorn and Gotzsche, Peter C. "Is the Placebo Powerless? An Analysis of Clinical Trials Comparing Placebo with No Treatment." The New England Journal of Medicine, May 24, 2001, Number 21, Volume 344:1594-1602.

74 Treisman, Michel. "Motion Sickness: An evolutionary hypothesis." *Science,* Volume 197, Issue 4302. 1977. Pp. 493-495.

75 Guthrie, Stewart (with Joseph Agassi, Karin R. Andriolo, David Buchdahl, H. Byron Earhart, Moshe Greenberg, Ian Jarvie, Benson Saler, John Saliba, Kevin J. Sharpe, Georges Tissot). "A Cognitive Theory of Religion." *Current Anthropology,* Vol. 21, No. 2, (Apr., 1980). P 190.

76 Wright, Robert. *The Moral Animal: Why We Are the Way We Are; The New Science of Evolutionary Psychology.* Vintage Books, 1994. p. 280.

77 Ross, Lee. "The intuitive psychologist and his shortcomings: Distortions in the attribution process." In L. Berkowitz (Ed.), *Advances in experimental social*

psychology (vol. 10). New York: Academic Press. 1977. P. 173–220

[78] Dawkins, Richard. *The Selfish Gene (30th Anniversary Edition).* Oxford University Press, 2006. P. xx.

[79] Wright, Robert. *The Moral Animal: Why We Are the Way We Are; The New Science of Evolutionary Psychology.* Vintage Books, 1994. p. 341.

[80] Wright, Robert. *The Moral Animal: Why We Are the Way We Are; The New Science of Evolutionary Psychology.* Vintage Books, 1994. p. 280.

[81] Wrangham, Richard, "Is Military Incompetence Adaptive?" Evolution and Human Behavior , 20 (1999). P. 10.

[82] Johnson, Dominic D. P., Fowler, James H. "The evolution of overconfidence." Nature 477, 317–320. September 14, 2011.

[83] Kahan, Dan M. and Peters, Ellen and Dawson, Erica Cantrell and Slovic, Paul, Motivated Numeracy and Enlightened Self-Government. September 3, 2013.

[84] Buss, David M. 1995. "Evolutionary Psychology: A New Paradigm for Psychological Science." Psychological Inquiry, 1995, Vol. 6, No. 1, p. 20.

[85] Dawkins, Richard. *The Selfish Gene* (30th Anniversary Edition). Oxford University Press, 2006. P. xx.

[86] Trivers, Robert. "The elements of a scientific theory of self-deception." Annals of the New York Academy of Sciences, 907. 2000. p. 119.

[87] Libet, Benjamin. "Neuronal time factors in conscious and unconscious mental functions." Toward a Science of Consciousness: The First Tucson Discussion and Debates. S. R. Hameroff, A.W. Kaszniak & A. Scott (Eds.). MIT Press. 1996. p. 337–347.

[88] Gazzaniga, Michael S. "The Split Brain Revisited." From "The Scientific American Book of the Brain." (ed. Antonio Damosio). The Lyons Press. 1999. p. 135

[89] Gazzaniga, Michael S. "The Split Brain Revisited." From "The Scientific American Book of the Brain." (ed. Antonio Damosio). The Lyons Press. 1999. p. 135-36.

[90] American Psychiatric Association. "Diagnostic criteria for 300.14 Dissociative Identity Disorder." *Diagnostic and Statistical Manual of Mental Disorders, Fourth Edition.* 2000

[91] Festinger, Leon, and Carlsmith, James M.. "Cognitive consequences of forced compliance." Journal of Abnormal and Social Psychology, 58, 1959. 203-211.

[92] Haidt, Jonathan and Kesebir, Selin. "Morality." (Final draft, submitted for copyediting). The Handbook of Social Psychology, 5th Edition, University of Virginia. S. T. Fiske & D. Gilbert (Eds.). March 21, 2009. p. 11.

[93] Foster, Kevin R. and Kokko, Hanna. "The evolution of superstitious and superstition-like behaviour." Proceedings of the Royal Society B. (2009) 276, p. 31.

[94] Shermer, Michael. "Patternicity: Finding Meaningful Patterns in Meaningless Noise: Why the brain believes something is real when it is not." Scientific American Magazine. December 2008.

[95] Spinoza, Baruch. *Ethics.* (translated from the Latin by R.H.M Elwes) 1677. Part IV: Of Human Bondage or the Strength of the Emotions, Preface.

[96] Boyer, Pascal. *Religion Explained: The Evolutionary Origins of Religions Thought.* Basic Books. 2001. P. 128.
[97] Vedantam, Shankar. "The Hidden Brain." Spiegel & Grau/The Random House Publishing Group. 2010. p. 153.
[98] Kessler, Michelle; Swartz, Jon; and Kirchhoff, Sue. "HP execs on spying: It wasn't me." USA Today, 9/29/2006
[99] From http://en.wikipedia.org/wiki/Religion, accessed February 7, 2011
[100] Boyer, Pascal. *Religion Explained: The Evolutionary Origins of Religions Thought.* Basic Books. 2001.
[101] Boyer, Pascal. *Religion Explained: The Evolutionary Origins of Religions Thought.* Basic Books. 2001. P. 49.
[102] Boyer, Pascal. *Religion Explained: The Evolutionary Origins of Religions Thought.* Basic Books. 2001. P. 28.
[103] Lloyd, Robin, "Metric mishap caused loss of NASA orbiter," CNN, September 30, 1999
[104] Schooler, Jonathan W.; Ohlsson, Stellan; Brooks, Kevin. "Thoughts Beyond Words: When Language Overshadows Insight." Journal of Experimental Psychology: General. Vol. 122, no. 2, 1993. p. 170.
[105] Schooler, Jonathan W.; Ryan, Robert S.; Reder, Lynne. "The Costs and Benefits of Verbally Rehearsing Memory for Faces." Basic and Applied Memory Research. Practical Applications. Volume 2 (Eds. Herrmann, Douglass et al.). Lawrence Erlbaum Associates, Inc. 1996. p. 60.
[106] Schooler, Jonathan W.; Ohlsson, Stellan; Brooks, Kevin. "Thoughts Beyond Words: When Language Overshadows Insight." Journal of Experimental Psychology: General. Vol. 122, no. 2, 1993. p. 169.
[107] Larson, Gary. *Night of the Crash-Test Dummies.* Andrews McMeel Publishing, 1988, p. 52.
[108] Boyer, Pascal. *Religion Explained: The Evolutionary Origins of Religions Thought.* Basic Books. 2001. P. 303.
[109] Boyer, Pascal. *Religion Explained: The Evolutionary Origins of Religions Thought.* Basic Books. 2001. P. 304.
[110] O.Neil, Robert M. (Chair) et al. "Report: Academic Freedom and Tenure. Savannah College of Art & Design." Academe: Bulletin of the AAUP. May-June 1993. P. 65-70.
[111] Benatar, Pat. "Evil Genius." Precious Time/Get Nervous. 1999.
[112] Amini, Adeel. "Minister of Magic: Adeel Amini delves into JK Rowling's chamber of secrets." Student, March 4, 2008.
[113] Davis, Hank. *Caveman Logic: The Persistence of Primitive Thinking in a Modern World.* Prometheus Books. 2009. P. 245.
[114] Davis, Hank. *Caveman Logic: The Persistence of Primitive Thinking in a Modern World.* Prometheus Books. 2009. P. 245-46.
[115] Hofstadter , Richard. *Anti-Intellectualism in American Life.* Knopf. 1963
[116] Pierce. Charles. *Idiot America: How Stupidity Became a Virtue in the Land of the Free.* Doubleday. 2009.
[117] Parks, Tim. "Booted: What Really Ails Italy/" *The New Yorker.* April 11, 2011.

P. 83.

[118] Clarke, Edward. *Sex in Education; Or, a Fair Chance for the Girls.* 1873. Note that the book was a best seller. Also, Clarke was a medical doctor and a member of the Harvard faculty.

[119] PwC. "Playing to win: The outlook for the global casino and online gaming market to 2014. 2010. P. 7.

[120] Pinker, Steven. *How the Mind Works.* W. W. Norton & Company. 2009. P. 346.

[121] Paumgarten, Nick. "Magic Mountain: What happens at Davos?" The New Yorker. March 5, 2012. P. 53.

[122] Hopkins, Claude. "Scientific Advertising." 1923. Chapter 1: How Advertising Laws Are Established; Part 2: The rules of advertising.

[123] Rifkin, Jeremy. *The Empathic Civilization.* Jeremy P. Tarcher/Penguin. 2009. p. 48.

[124] Day, Ruth S. "Comprehension of Prescription Drug Information: Overview of A Research Program." Technical Report SS-06-01 (Papers from the 2006 AAAI Spring Symposium). Published by The AAAI Press, Menlo Park, California. p. 24

[125] Mack, John. "DTC Pros and Cons Presented at FDA Hearing." Pharma Marketing News. Volume 4, Number 10. VirSci Corporation. November 2005.

[126] Political Economy Research Institute. *Toxic 100 Air Polluters.* http://www.peri.umass.edu/toxic_index/. March 2010.

[127] Greenpeace USA. "Koch Industries Secretly Funding the Climate Denial Machine." March 2010. P. 6.

[128] Koch Industries, Inc. http://www.kochind.com/viewpoint/ (Accessed May 2011).

[129] Mayer, Jane. "Covert Operations: The billionaire brothers who are waging a war against Obama." *The New Yorker.* August 30, 2010.

[130] Anonymous. "Rogues of K Street: Confessions of a Tea Party Consultant." *Playboy.* July 2010.

[131] Wright, Robert. *The Moral Animal: Why We Are the Way We Are; The New Science of Evolutionary Psychology.* Vintage Books, 1994. p. 84.

[132] Dawkins, Richard, *The God Delusion.* First Mariner Books (Houghton Mifflin Co.), 2008. page 405.

[133] Dawkins, Richard, *The God Delusion.* First Mariner Books (Houghton Mifflin Co.), 2008. p. 331.

[134] Dawkins, Richard, *The God Delusion.* First Mariner Books (Houghton Mifflin Co.), 2008. p. 201.

[135] Pinker, Steven. *How the Mind Works.* W. W. Norton & Company. 2009. P. 52.

www.ingramcontent.com/pod-product-compliance
Lightning Source LLC
Chambersburg PA
CBHW060506030426
42337CB00015B/1772